Vegetables
FOR ALL SEASONS

COMPILED BY JENNENE PLUMMER

PHOTOGRAPHY BY
QUENTIN BACON AND ASHLEY BARBER

BayBooks
An imprint of HarperCollinsPublishers

ACKNOWLEDGEMENT:

Yvonne Webb for the following recipes:

Piroshki
Marinated Fish with Carrots
Potato Patties
Radishes with Sour Cream
Cabbage Rolls
Stuffed Summer Squash
Red Cabbage with Sour Cream
Stuffed Green Peppers
Dill Tomato
Pickled Cauliflower
Sweet Corn Strudel

A Bay Books Publication

Bay Books, an imprint of
HarperCollins*Publishers*
25 Ryde Road, Pymble, Sydney, NSW, 2073, Australia
Distributed in the United States of America by
HarperCollins Publishers
10 East 53rd Street, New York NY 10022, USA

First published in Australia in 1992
Revised edition published in Australia in 1993
This edition published in the USA in 1995

ISBN 1 86378 252 4

Cover and chapter opening photography by Quentin Bacon
with stylist Jennene Plummer

Printed in China
5 4 3 2 1
99 98 97 96 95

CONTENTS
~

VEGETABLES FOR ALL SEASONS ~ 4

VEGETABLE KNOW HOW ~ 6

FLOWER CROPS ~ 8

PEAS, BEANS & PULSES ~ 18

SWEET CORN ~ 28

ROOT CROPS ~ 30

MUSHROOMS ~ 42

LEAFY CROPS ~ 46

CROPS FROM VINES ~ 58

SWEET VEGETABLES ~ 68

ONIONS & OTHER ALLIUMS ~ 70

FRUITS OF THE EARTH ~ 80

GROWING YOUR OWN ~ 90

INDEX ~ 94

VEGETABLES FOR ALL SEASONS

Vegetables provide an endless variety of flavors, textures, colors and shapes to add interest to every meal, every day. Nowadays, vegetable cookery is becoming more and more popular with the discovery that these delectable foods are more than mere accompaniments, they are a meal in themselves. And the nutrition experts tell us we should eat more of them. In addition, a wider range of vegetables than ever before is readily available.

In *Vegetables for all Seasons*, we have included recipes for all types of vegetables from the humble and ever popular potato to the more exotic artichoke. Although we have emphasized vegetables that are widely available, we have also included recipes for some of the more unusual items found in the marketplace.

Be adventurous. These new or more unusual vegetables are an easy way to bring variety to family meals. Red lettuce adds interest to eye and palate; sprouts enliven salad days; watercress is delicious on its own, added to soups and stews, or as a garnish with meat or chicken meals; fennel can be served raw in salads, or added to soups. Its aromatic aniseed taste is unmistakable. Belgian endive (witloof) has a slightly bitter flavor but combines well with salad ingredients and fruit.

Try baby vegetables. Miniature carrots, beets, cauliflower, zucchini and corn are now available. You can steam, sauté, stir-fry or microwave them whole with very little waste.

Chinese cabbages and green vegetables are increasingly popular. Tempt the family tastebuds, and steam, microwave or stir-fry bok choy's ivory white stalks and green leaves, Peking cabbage with its broad-ribbed, yellow-white leaf stalks and crinkly leaves or Chinese flowering cabbage with its yellow flowers and green leaf stems.

Kale, another member of the cabbage family, is rich in vitamins A and C and is a good source of calcium. Looking like a large parsley plant with its dark curly green leaves, it's simply delicious steamed or microwaved and served with freshly squeezed lemon juice and a twist of freshly ground black pepper.

Kohlrabi, another newcomer, comes with green or purple skin, white flesh, and has shoots all over it. Try kohlrabi: grated over salads, steamed, microwaved, sautéed, or used in recipes as a substitute for turnips.

Although sophisticated growing methods, refrigerated transport and cold storage have made it possible to buy most vegetables all year round, they are still of the best quality, value and flavor when in season. Always choose vegetables that are not discolored, damaged, limp or wilting. Wash them carefully, particularly the leafy varieties, before serving. Never soak them, chop them excessively or overcook them, as nutrients are lost in all of these ways.

Nutritional Know How

Most people know that vegetables are good for you; few realize just what an essential role they play in our everyday health and well-being and in preventing disease. As a group, vegetables are:

• Low in fat

• Low in sodium

• Low in calories.

They are also good sources for:

• Vitamin C

• Vitamin A (as beta carotene)

• Folacin

• Dietary fiber.

For vitamin C eat plenty of tomatoes, red and green peppers, broccoli, cauliflower, Brussels sprouts and cabbage. Vitamin C is destroyed by heat (cooking), light and oxygen (cut surfaces). It is also water soluble which means that it can be lost if you soak vegetables in water. To retain vitamin C, do not overcook vegetables, do not cut vegetables into tiny pieces to save cooking time, and use as little water as possible when cooking. Quickly steaming, microwaving and sautéing are the best ways to retain vitamin C in vegetables. Did you know that vitamin C helps your body to absorb iron?

The best sources of Vitamin A are dark green, yellow and orange vegetables. Carrots, pumpkin, spinach and broccoli are all excellent. Color is the clue to beta carotene. Did you know that red peppers have up to seven times more vitamin A than green?

Most vegetables are high in dietary fiber, particularly soluble fiber. Potatoes, carrots, parsnips, tomatoes, spinach, peas, corn, broccoli and cauliflower are all good sources of dietary fiber. Vegetables with edible skins have a higher fiber content if you prepare and eat them with the skin left on. Simply scrub the skins of potatoes or pumpkins with a soft brush to remove dirt. Did you

know that leaving the skin on not only increases fiber, it helps retain flavor, vitamins and minerals?

Eating plenty of vegetables every day can keep you healthy, keep you slim, reduce your blood pressure level, reduce your blood cholesterol level and improve diabetic control. You should aim to eat at least 2 cups or 5 servings of vegetables every day. (An average adult serving is 1 medium-sized potato or 1 to 2 well-rounded tablespoons of cooked vegetables.) You can achieve this by serving more vegetables with your evening meal, munching salad or salad sandwiches for lunch and crunching raw vegetable snacks such as baby carrots, celery stalks or slices of red and green pepper when you feel hungry in-between times.

VEGETABLE KNOW HOW

VEGETABLE	PREPARATION	FREEZING	MICROWAVE Cook vegetables at 100% power and always cover with lid or plastic wrap.
ARTICHOKES	• Place upside down in salted water to dislodge any hidden insects or earth. Trim stem and tough outer leaves. Snip sharp points from leaves. Brush any cut surfaces with lemon juice to prevent discoloration.	• Remove tough outer leaves, trim and remove choke. Blanch 7 minutes in water with lemon juice. Drain upside down. Pack in rigid containers.	• 4 small artichokes, 7 to 9 minutes; large or globe, 15 minutes (stand 3 to 4 minutes)
ASPARAGUS	• Bend lower end of stalk between thumb and forefinger to break off woody end.	• Blanch 2 to 4 minutes, depending on thickness of stalk. Pack between sheets of freezer wrap.	• 1 lb, 4 minutes (stand 1 to 2 minutes)
BEANS	• All beans need to be trimmed. Some varieties such as runner beans will also need their strings removed. Beans can then be sliced or left whole.	• Blanch 1 to 2 minutes. Pack into freezer bags.	• 1 lb, 6 to 8 minutes with 2 tablespoons water (stand 1 to 2 minutes)
BEETS	• Trim tops. To prevent 'bleeding' during cooking, don't peel beforehand. Scrub gently with a soft brush.	• Blanch 2 to 3 minutes. Pack in freezer bags.	• 1lb, 12 to 17 minutes (stand 5 minutes)
BELGIAN ENDIVE (WITLOOF)	• Remove any damaged outer leaves, trim base.	• Do not freeze.	• 4 endive, 13 to 14 minutes
BROCCOLI	• Trim stems. Divide into even florets. Peel stems and cut in pieces. Rinse in cold water.	• Blanch 1 to 2 minutes. Pack in layers between sheets of freezer wrap.	• 1lb, 6 to 8 minutes (stand 1 to 2 minutes)
BRUSSELS SPROUTS	• Trim base and tough outer leaves. Cut a cross in stem end.	• Blanch 1 to 2 minutes. Pack into freezer bags.	• 1 pint, 3 minutes; 1lb, 4 to 5 minutes (stand 1 to 2 minutes)
CABBAGE	• Trim tough and damaged outer leaves. Remove core and hard ribs. Rinse, chop or shred.	• Blanch 1 minute. Pack into freezer bags.	• 1 lb shredded, 3 to 5 minutes; whole, 5 minutes (stand 1 to 2 minutes)
CARROTS	• Trim and scrub - young carrots do not require peeling. Slice, dice, or cut into julienne strips; leave young carrots whole.	• Blanch 1 to 2 minutes. Pack into freezer bags.	• 1 lb, 5 to 6 minutes; whole, 8 minutes (stand 1 minute)
CAULIFLOWER	• Remove leaves, wash. Cut into even florets.	• Blanch 1 to 2 minutes. Pack into freezer bags or in rigid containers between sheets of freezer wrap.	• 1 lb, 6 to 8 minutes (stand 1 to 2 minutes)
CELERY	• Separate stalks, trim top and base. Remove strings if necessary. Slice as required.	• Blanch 1 minute. Pack into freezer bags.	• 1 lb, 4 to 5 minutes (stand 1 to 2 minutes)

VEGETABLE	PREPARATION	FREEZING	MICROWAVE Cook vegetables at 100% power and always cover with lid or plastic wrap.
EGGPLANT	• Remove stem, halve, slice or dice. Sprinkle with salt, leave 30 minutes. Rinse and pat dry.	• Blanch 2 minutes. Pack into rigid containers.	• 1 lb whole, 5 to 6 minutes (stand 1 to 2 minutes)
FENNEL	• Trim root and top leaves. Remove and discard any discoloured outer sheaths. Halve or slice.	• Blanch 1 minute. Pack in rigid container in blanching water.	• 1 lb, 5 minutes (stand 2 minutes)
LEEKS	• Trim roots and tops. Wash very well. Leave whole or slice.	• Slice finely, blanch 1 minute. Pack in freezer bags.	• 1 lb sliced, 6 minutes (stand 1 to 2 minutes)
MUSHROOMS	• Wipe with a damp cloth. Trim stalks if necessary.	• Blanch 30 seconds. Drain. Open freeze then store in freezer bags.	• 1 lb sliced, 4 to 5 minutes; whole caps, 12 minutes (stand 1 to 2 minutes)
OKRA	• Wash, scrub off 'fuzz'. Leave whole or slice.	• Do not freeze. (But commercially frozen oka is available.)	• 1 lb, 6 to 10 minutes (stand 1 to 2 minutes)
ONIONS	• Remove skins. Halve, quarter, dice or slice.	• Chop, double wrap and pack in freezer bags.	• 1 lb sliced, 4 to 5 minutes
PARSNIPS	• Scrape, peel. Halve lengthwise, slice or cut into chunks. If very large remove core.	• Slice or dice. Blanch 1 minute. Pack into freezer bags.	• 1 lb, 8 minutes with 1 cup water (stand 1 to 2 minutes)
PEAS	• Shell and rinse.	• Blanch 30 seconds to 1 minute. Pack into freezer bags.	• ½ lb shelled, 5 to 8 minutes (stand 1 to 2 minutes)
PEPPERS	• Cut off top, remove seeds, core and membrane. Cube or slice.	• Blanch 1 to 2 minutes. Pack into freezer bags.	• 1 lb sliced, 2 to 3 minutes (stand 1 minute)
POTATOES	• Wash and scrub or peel. Slice as required.	• Blanch 1 to 2 minutes. Pack into freezer bags.	• 1 lb, 8 to 10 minutes; 2 baking potatoes, 12 to 15 minutes (stand 2 to 3 minutes)
PUMPKIN	• Wash, cut into pieces. Remove seeds and skin (if desired).	• Cut into serving size pieces. Pack into freezer bags.	• 1 lb, 8 to 10 minutes (stand 1 to 2 minutes)
SPINACH	• Separate stem from leaves. Shred.	• Blanch 1 minute. Squeeze out as much liquid as possible. Pack into freezer bags.	• 1 lb, 3 to 4 minutes (stand 1 to 2 minutes)
SNOW PEAS	• Top and tail. Remove strings.	• Blanch 30 seconds to 1 minute. Pack into freezer bags.	• 1 lb, 2 to 3 minutes (stand 1 minute)
SWEET CORN	• Leave husk on if microwaving, and remove silk when done. Or husk can be completely removed before cooking.	• Blanch 2 minutes. Wrap individually. Pack into freezer bags.	• Each ear, 2 to 3 minutes; 4 ears, 9 minutes (stand 1 to 2 minutes)
SQUASH, WINTER	• Trim. Leave whole, halve, quarter or slice.	• Blanch 1 minute. Pack into freezer bags.	• 1 lb, 7 minutes (stand 1 minute)
SWISS CHARD	• Separate white stem from green leaves. Shred.	• Blanch 1 minute. Squeeze out as much liquid as possible. Pack into freezer bag.	• 1 lb, 3 to 4 minutes (stand 1 to 2 minutes)
ZUCCHINI AND SUMMER SQUASH	• Wash and trim ends. Leave whole, cut into halves or slices.	• Cut into slices. Blanch 1 minute. Pack into freezer bags.	• 1 lb sliced, 4 to 5 minutes; whole, 10 minutes (stand 1 minute)

FLOWER CROPS

Cauliflower and broccoli are descendants of the wild cabbage. Look for firm, unblemished florets when shopping and separate into even-sized florets to cook, washing well before steaming, microwaving or stir-frying until tender. They are also delicious raw or blanched in salads or eaten with a dip.

Asparagus is a stalk vegetable with an exquisite flavor. The thickness of the stem bears no relationship to tenderness. Wash well and cook until just tender. Serve with melted butter and a little Parmesan cheese or create wonderful soups, salads and soufflés.

The globe artichoke (not to be confused with the Jerusalem artichoke) is a thistle. The tender heart is found at the base of the artichoke. Dip the tender base of the cooked leaves in a sauce or dressing. Add the hearts to salads or serve with pasta.

Celery is available year round and is equally delicious cooked in stir-fries, soups and stews or crunched raw in salads.

GREEN SALAD PRIMAVERA

½ pound fresh spinach spirali
or ⅓ package dried

¼ pound shelled fresh green peas

¼ pound small green beans

½ pound asparagus cut into 2-inch lengths

½ pound broccoli florets

2 small zucchini sliced diagonally

½ cup snow peas

½ cup button mushrooms, halved

¼ cup olive oil

2 tablespoons fresh lemon juice

1 teaspoon Dijon mustard

1 tablespoon finely chopped fresh tarragon
or ½ teaspoon dried steeped in 1 teaspoon
olive oil for 45 minutes

freshly ground black pepper

1 Blanch green vegetables, refresh under cold water and drain.

2 Cook pasta in boiling salted water until *al dente* (see Note). Drain, rinse under cold water and drain again. Transfer to a bowl. Stir through a little olive oil to prevent the pasta from sticking together.

3 Add blanched vegetables and mushrooms to pasta.

4 Combine oil, lemon juice, mustard, tarragon and pepper. Pour dressing over vegetables. Toss lightly to coat. Can be served immediately, but is better if refrigerated for 1 to 2 hours first.

NOTE: *al dente* means 'to the tooth'. Pasta should be tender with a slightly firmer center.

SERVES 4 TO 6

Green Salad Primavera

CAULIFLOWER AND BROCCOLI SALAD

1 pound cauliflower

1 pound broccoli

1 cup vinaigrette dressing

1 to 2 teaspoons Dijon mustard

1 teaspoon capers, chopped

Tabasco sauce, to taste

paprika, to taste

1 Wash cauliflower and broccoli. Separate into florets. Cook broccoli and cauliflower separately until tender but still crisp. Drain and cool.

2 Combine dressing with mustard, capers and Tabasco sauce.

3 Arrange vegetables in a serving dish. Pour over dressing and lightly toss. Cover and chill. Serve sprinkled with paprika.

SERVES 10 TO 12

CAULIFLOWER AND MACARONI SOUFFLÉ

1 medium cauliflower, cut into florets

5 eggs, separated

2 teaspoons prepared mustard

freshly ground black pepper, to taste

1 cup white sauce

1 cup grated tasty cheese

1 cup cooked elbow macaroni

1 Cook cauliflower in water until tender. Drain well. Process in a food processor or blender until smooth with egg yolks, mustard and seasonings.

2 TO PREPARE WHITE SAUCE: Melt 2 tablespoons butter or margarine in a small saucepan. Blend in 3 tablespoons flour. Cook 1 minute. Remove from heat. Blend in 1 cup milk. Return to heat. Cook, stirring constantly, until sauce boils and thickens. Simmer for 3 minutes. Season to taste.

3 Add cheese to white sauce. Cool and add sauce to purée. Blend in macaroni.

4 Beat egg whites until stiff peaks form. Fold gently into cauliflower mixture. Spoon into large greased soufflé dish. Bake in a moderately hot oven 375°F for 35 minutes or until set. Serve immediately with salad and crusty bread.

SERVES 4 TO 6

BROCCOLI WITH HORSERADISH

6 tablespoons butter or margarine, melted

¾ cup mayonnaise

3 tablespoons horseradish

1 small onion, finely chopped

¼ teaspoon dry mustard

freshly ground black pepper

paprika

1 large bunch fresh broccoli or 2 packets frozen

1½ tablespoons lemon juice

2 tablespoons butter or margarine

1 Combine melted butter, mayonnaise, horseradish, onion, mustard and seasoning. Chill until required.

2 Cook broccoli until crisp but tender. Drain. Refresh in cold water. Reheat with a little lemon and butter. Serve hot with sauce.

SERVES 8

 **BROCCOLI STEMS**

Broccoli stems may be peeled using a sharp knife to ensure that they cook in the same time as the tender florets. If desired, the thicker lower parts can also be peeled and sliced into short lengths before cooking and will take the same time as the stems.

TOMATO FETTUCCINE WITH CAULIFLOWER AND OLIVES

½ medium cauliflower

4 tomatoes, peeled and chopped

½ cup olive oil

1 clove garlic, crushed

30 stuffed olives

½ pound tomato fettuccine
noodles

2 ounces ham, diced

½ cup Parmesan or Pecorino
cheese

1 Break cauliflower into florets. Cook in boiling water until tender but still crisp. Drain well.

2 Simmer tomatoes, olive oil and garlic over medium heat for 10 minutes. Add olives. Set aside.

3 Cook fettuccine in boiling water until *al dente*. Drain well. Divide among individual plates.

4 Combine tomato mixture, cauliflower and ham and reheat gently. Spoon over the fettuccine. Sprinkle with cheese and serve hot.

SERVES 6

PICKLED CAULIFLOWER

1 large cauliflower

PICKLING MIXTURE

3½ cups water

1 cup vinegar

1 cup sugar

1 tablespoon salt

10 peppercorns

3 bay leaves

2 cloves

1 Break cauliflower into florets. Rinse, blanch, drain and cool.

2 TO PREPARE PICKLING MIXTURE: Combine all ingredients in a large saucepan. Bring to the boil. Cook, stirring continuously, until sugar dissolves. Set mixture aside to cool.

3 Place cauliflower in suitable glass or earthenware container. Pour pickling mixture over it. Cover container. Label and store in a cool place or in the refrigerator. It should be ready to eat in 2 to 3 days.

SERVES 6 TO 8

SCALLOP AND ASPARAGUS BOUCHÉE

2 tablespoons butter or margarine

12 button mushrooms, sliced

3 tablespoons finely chopped
scallions

¾ cup dry vermouth or dry white
wine

4 large (sea) scallops, trimmed

¾ cup heavy cream

1 tablespoon butter or margarine
blended with 2 teaspoons
plain flour

12 asparagus spears, trimmed

1 tablespoon lemon juice

freshly ground black pepper,
to taste

6 puff pastry cases

watercress sprigs and lemon slices,
to garnish

1 Cook mushrooms gently in butter until tender. Set aside.

2 Sauté scallions in same pan over a low heat until tender. Blend in the wine. Add scallops. Simmer 1 to 2 minutes. Remove scallops and slice.

3 Simmer liquid in pan until reduced by one-third. Add cream and continue

simmering until reduced slightly. Stir in blended flour and butter, until smooth and thickened.

4 Cook asparagus in boiling water until just becoming tender. Refresh under cold water. Drain well. Cut tips from asparagus and set aside for garnish.

5 Purée the stalks with lemon juice and seasoning in a food processor. Add asparagus purée to cream sauce, together with mushrooms and scallops. Heat through without boiling.

6 Heat pastry cases in a moderate oven 350°F for 10 minutes. Place on serving plates, fill with hot scallop mixture.

Arrange asparagus tips on top. Garnish with watercress and a slice of lemon.

SERVES 6

Tomato Fettuccine with Cauliflower and Olives

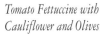

STEP-BY-STEP TECHNIQUES

STUFFED GLOBE ARTICHOKES

4 globe artichokes

4 lemon slices

3 tablespoons white vinegar

6 hard-boiled eggs, chopped

3 scallions, chopped

5 tomatoes, peeled, seeded and chopped

DRESSING

⅔ cup yogurt

1 tablespoon oil

1 teaspoon honey

1 teaspoon Dijon mustard

1 lemon, juiced

1 tablespoon chopped parsley

1 Remove stems from artichokes. Cut slice from top. Trim leaves and rub with cut lemon. Stand each on a slice of lemon in a saucepan. Cook in boiling water with vinegar for 15 to 20 minutes. (Do not use an aluminum pot.) Drain.

2 TO PREPARE DRESSING: Shake all ingredients together in a screw-top jar until well blended.

3 Mix dressing with eggs, scallions and tomatoes to make filling.

4 Gently open artichoke leaves to reveal center hairy choke. Scoop this out with a teaspoon and discard. Spoon filling into center.

SERVES 4

Stand artichokes on slices of lemon and cook in boiling water.

Spoon filling into artichokes.

Stuffed Globe Artichokes

WHOLE WHEAT SALAD TARTLETS

PASTRY

1¼ cups sifted flour

1 cup whole wheat flour

1 tablespoon chopped herbs

¼ pound butter or margarine, cut in small pieces

1 egg yolk

3 tablespoons lemon juice

freshly ground black pepper

ice water

FILLING

1 cup chopped tomatoes

½ cup canned asparagus pieces

¼ cup steamed peas

¼ cup chopped celery

¼ cup grated carrot

¼ cup corn kernels

3 tablespoons chopped chives

plain yogurt

1 TO PREPARE PASTRY: Place flours and herbs in bowl. Rub in butter using fingertips. Add egg yolk, lemon juice, seasoning and enough water to form a dough. Wrap in plastic wrap. Refrigerate for 30 minutes.

2 Knead dough on a lightly floured board until smooth. Roll pastry to ¼-inch thickness. Cut out with 3-inch round cutter. Place in tartlet pans. Bake 10 minutes in a hot oven 400°F until golden. Cool.

3 TO PREPARE FILLING: Combine all vegetables. Stir in enough yogurt to hold filling together. Spoon into baked pastry shells. Chill thoroughly before serving.

MAKES 12

ASPARAGUS WITH HERBS AND PARMESAN

16 thick asparagus spears

6 tablespoons butter or margarine

1 clove garlic, finely chopped

1 tablespoon finely chopped fresh parsley

1 tablespoon finely chopped chives

1 tablespoon lemon juice

grated Parmesan cheese

1 Break off woody ends of the asparagus, and peel the lower part of the stalks. Wash the asparagus well in cold running water. Tie into 2 bundles with string. Place in an asparagus steamer or a large pan of boiling water. The stalks only should be in the water so that the tips steam.

2 Cover the pan with foil or an upturned saucepan of the same diameter. Cook for 5 to 7 minutes, depending on the thickness of the asparagus. Test after 4 minutes (the thickest part of the stalk should be just tender). Overcooking ruins asparagus.

3 Drain well. Keep warm. Melt the butter in a small frying pan over medium heat. Add the garlic and cook gently for a minute. Stir in the herbs and lemon juice.

4 Place asparagus on warmed plates. Pour over the sauce. Serve Parmesan separately.

SERVES 4

 WATCH THE WATER

When boiling vegetables always use a minimum of water as the more water used increases vitamin loss.

 CRISP BUT TENDER

Cauliflower and broccoli are easily ruined if overcooked. They should be tender but still slightly crisp. A way to help prevent overcooking is to turn the heat off 5 minutes before the end of cooking time.

Au Gratin

Cooked cauliflower and broccoli are delicious when served au gratin, i.e., covered with a white sauce, topped with shredded tasty cheese and bread crumbs and baked in a moderate oven 350°F until the topping is golden.

Inner Greens

The inner green leaves of the cauliflower may be boiled and eaten as a delicious accompaniment to a main meal.

MIDDLE EASTERN PILAF

5 tablespoons oil

3 stalks celery, chopped into small pieces

2 large onions, peeled and chopped

2 cloves garlic, crushed

½ cup seedless raisins

½ cup currants

¼ cup shelled pistachio nuts

½ cup pine nuts

2 cups long grain rice

4½ cups boiling water

freshly ground black pepper

sour cream or yogurt

1 Heat half the oil in a large fry pan. Sauté celery and onions for 2 minutes. Add garlic, raisins, currants and nuts. Cook, stirring, for 3 minutes.

2 Remove ingredients with slotted spoon. Set aside. Add remaining oil to same pan. When hot add rice. Stir for a few minutes until rice begins to turn milky.

3 Pour in boiling water. Add seasoning. Cover pan. Cook until water is absorbed, fluffing occasionally. Stir in onion and fruit mixture. Serve with a dollop of sour cream or yogurt.

SERVES 4

CELERY CREAM SOUP

4 tablespoons butter or margarine

3 onions, peeled and chopped

1 bunch celery, chopped

7 cups beef stock

1⅓ cups heavy cream

freshly ground black pepper

celery seeds, for garnish

1 Melt butter in a large saucepan. Sauté onions and celery until onions are transparent.

2 Stir in beef stock. Simmer 45 minutes. Blend until smooth in food processor. This may be done in several batches.

3 Add cream and seasoning. Reheat (without boiling). Sprinkle lightly with celery seeds to serve.

SERVES 4 TO 6

SESAME BRAISED CELERY

½ bunch celery, sliced diagonally

1 tablespoon oil

1 teaspoon sesame oil

½ red pepper, cut into thin strips

1 clove garlic, crushed

toasted sesame seeds for serving

1 Blanch celery and pepper. Drain well.

2 Heat oils in a skillet. Cook garlic briefly. Add celery and pepper over high heat stirring constantly 4 to 6 minutes.

3 Transfer to a serving dish. Serve sprinkled with toasted sesame seeds.

SERVES 2

ARTICHOKE AND DRY SAUSAGE FETTUCCINE

¼ pound mild salami, julienned

1 onion, chopped

2 cloves garlic, crushed

1 cup chicken stock

½ cup dry white wine

One 6-ounce jar artichoke hearts, drained and quartered

½ pound fettuccine

4 tablespoons butter or margarine

freshly ground black pepper to taste

½ cup Parmesan cheese

3 tablespoons finely chopped parsley

½ red pepper, cut into strips

1 Combine salami, onion and garlic in a frying pan. Cook gently until the onion is golden. Pour in stock and wine.

2 Bring to the boil then simmer, covered, for 15 minutes. Add the artichoke hearts and cook until heated through. Set aside the covered pan.

3 Cook fettuccine in plenty of boiling water until *al dente*. Drain and toss with butter and seasoning. Combine fettuccine with the artichoke mixture.

4 Serve in individual portions sprinkled with Parmesan cheese and parsley. Garnish with pepper strips.

SERVES 6

Artichoke and Dry Sausage Fettuccine

PEAS, BEANS & PULSES

Peas, snow peas, green beans, broad beans, long beans and a variety of dried beans and lentils (pulses) are featured in this chapter.

Snow peas are so tender and delicate that they are eaten shell and all! They are wider and thinner than other peas and best served crisp — either blanch them or lightly stir-fry. Available all year, look for crisp, bright green snow peas and avoid those that are shriveled, dull or have brown spots.

Green beans, whether elegant haricot vert or simple bush beans, are slender and crisp. You can tell a good bean if it snaps easily when broken. Look for bright, blemish-free beans.

Peas are sweet and delicate in flavor and can be used in a great variety of dishes. Look for peas with bright green shiny pods.

Bean sprouts, a traditional ingredient in Asian cuisine, are great in stir-fries or raw in salads. Choose white crisp sprouts and eat as fresh as possible.

Vegetable Pâté

VEGETABLE PÂTÉ

*This pâté is delicious served with a sauce made
from onions, garlic and tomatoes.*

1 leek, well washed

2 cups shelled peas

2 pounds finely chopped spinach

1 egg

½ teaspoon dried tarragon

¼ teaspoon nutmeg

1 pound sliced carrots

freshly ground black pepper to taste

4 tablespoons butter or margarine

½ cup water

3 tablespoons flour

1 Slice the white part of the leek into thin
rounds. Steam until tender. Line a loaf pan
with oiled wax paper. Place the cooked leek
on the bottom, smoothing it down to make
a thin layer.

2 Cook the peas in boiling water and steam
the spinach over them. When the peas are
tender, drain and combine with the spinach,
egg, tarragon and nutmeg in a food
processor or blender. Process until puréed.

3 Spoon the purée over the leeks. Smooth
out the top with a spatula.

4 Cook the carrots with pepper, butter
and water until they are tender. Drain off
any remaining liquid. Purée the carrots
with the flour in a food processor
or blender.

5 Spoon the carrot purée over the spinach
in the loaf pan. Smooth the top with a
spatula. Tap the sides of the pan to remove
any air bubbles.

6 Place wax paper over the pâté, then cover
with 3 to 4 layers of foil. Bake in a moderate
oven 350°F for 1½ hours. Allow the pâté
to chill for 2 hours before turning out onto
a serving dish.

SERVES 4

MINESTRONE SOUP

⅓ cup dried cannellini or any small white beans

⅓ cup whole dried peas

10 cups chicken or vegetable stock

2 medium carrots, sliced

1 large stick celery, chopped

1 large onion, sliced

2 tomatoes, peeled and quartered

½ cup any leafy green vegetable, sliced

½ teaspoon dried basil

½ teaspoon dried oregano

½ cup macaroni

½ cup grated Parmesan cheese

chopped parsley to garnish

1 Pick over, then soak the beans and peas together overnight in 3 cups of stock. The beans should be white and plump, the peas green and plump. Discard any that are hard, brown or wrinkled.

2 Add the peas, beans and their soaking stock to the remaining stock with the carrots, celery and onion in a large pan. Bring to the boil. Simmer for 1 to 2 hours or until the beans and peas are tender.

3 Add the tomatoes, leafy vegetable, basil and oregano. Cook for 10 minutes.

4 Stir in macaroni. Cook for 10 to 15 minutes until it is tender. Serve sprinkled with grated cheese and parsley. Accompany with crusty bread.

SERVES 6

 PEAS IN THE POD

Remove peas from pod by pressing seam to cause it to split. Frozen peas are a wonderful substitute and time-saver for today's busy lifestyle.

SPLIT PEA AND HAM SOUP

1 pound green split peas

3 quarts water

2 ham shanks (optional)

½ pound ham or neck bones

3 leeks, thinly sliced or 2 medium-sized white onions, peeled and sliced

3 medium-sized potatoes, peeled and diced

1 stalk celery, chopped

1 Soak peas in enough water to cover overnight. Drain well. Place in a large pan with the water, ham shanks and ham or neck bones. Bring to boil. Reduce heat and simmer slowly for 3 hours.

2 Add leeks, potatoes and celery. Simmer for another 30 minutes, stirring occasionally. Remove meat from ham shanks. Discard all bones. Serve with hot crusty bread.

NOTE: This soup may be puréed if preferred.

SERVES 8

 PRESSURE COOKER

A pressure cooker may also be used to cook pulses and no soaking is required before.

Minestrone Soup

DUCK AND MANGO COMBINATION

This salad is best prepared as close to serving time as possible.

4 to 5 pound duck or 2 cups cooked duck meat

freshly ground pepper

1 pound green beans, sliced

2 red peppers, cut in strips

1 mango, peeled and chopped

½ cup shelled macadamia nuts

½ pound fresh or canned lychees, halved

½ cup olive oil

¼ cup lemon juice

1 Wash and dry duck. Season inside and out with pepper. Prick the skin with a fork to drain off fat during cooking. Truss and place on a rack in a roasting dish. Roast at 350°F for 2 hours or until tender and cooked when tested. Drain fat from pan as necessary.
2 Discard trussing strings, and roast an additional 10 minutes. Remove from oven and allow to cool. Cut off meat, discard skin fat and bones, and cut into bite-sized pieces. Set aside.
3 Drop beans into boiling water, then simmer uncovered, until just tender. Refresh under cold running water and drain.
4 Blanch peppers in boiling water. Refresh under cold running water, and drain.
5 Just before serving, combine all ingredients in a bowl. Toss until well mixed. Serve at room temperature.

SERVES 8 TO 10

STRING BEANS WITH ALMONDS

1 pound string beans, sliced

5 tablespoons toasted, slivered almonds

butter or margarine to serve

Place beans and almonds in a steamer. Secure lid. Steam for 6 minutes. Serve with dobs of butter.

SERVES 4

CELERY AND KIDNEY BEAN SALAD

1 can kidney beans, drained

2 cups chopped celery

1 small onion, finely chopped

½ cup chopped walnuts

5 tablespoons oil

¼ cup red wine vinegar

pepper, to taste

Combine beans with celery, onions and nuts. Whisk together oil, vinegar and seasoning. Pour over beans mixture. Serve chilled in lettuce cups.

SERVES 4 TO 6

SNOW PEA AND SEAFOOD TEMPURA

1 pound raw shrimp

½ pound snapper fillets

¼ pound snow peas

oil for deep frying

BATTER

½ cup flour

½ cup cornstarch

1½ teaspoons baking powder

1 egg

1 cup ice water

 GREEN BEANS

To keep beans and peas green, boil without a lid and drain them as soon as they are cooked. Also, never overcook them as this will cause loss of color.

DIPPING SAUCE

2 cups dashi (see Note)

3 tablespoons rice wine or dry sherry

1 to 3 tablespoons soy sauce

1 tablespoon finely grated daikon, for garnish

2 teaspoons grated fresh ginger, for garnish

1 Shell and devein shrimp. Skin snapper fillets, check for bones and cut into strips. String snow peas if necessary.

2 TO PREPARE BATTER: Sift flour, cornstarch and baking powder into a chilled bowl. Beat the egg and water together. Pour gradually into flour mixture and whisk gently to combine. Do not overmix. Add one ice cube to mixture to help keep cold.

3 TO PREPARE DIPPING SAUCE: Combine dashi, rice wine and soy sauce. Heat gently while frying tempura.

4 Heat oil to 350°F. Dip shrimp, fish and snow peas into batter one piece at a time. Drain off excess batter. Cook a few pieces at a time in oil until light golden in color. Drain well on absorbent paper. Arrange decoratively on a serving plate.

5 Serve hot dipping sauce in individual bowls, with 1 teaspoon grated daikon and ½ teaspoon ginger in each bowl.

NOTE: Dashi powder or paste is available from most Asian groceries and many supermarkets.

SERVES 4

Duck and Mango Combination

 TEMPURA

The batter for tempura should be light, crisp and thin, so that the food shows through the cooked batter. Tempura is served with a dipping sauce garnished with white radish (daikon) and fresh ginger.

Herbed Green Beans

MUSSELS AND SNOW PEAS

2 pounds mussels

1 cup water

½ pound snow peas, trimmed

10 to 12 fresh lychees, peeled

4 slices ginger root, peeled and finely sliced

½ cup Tomato Dressing (see recipe below)

1 Scrub mussels and remove beards. Discard any mussels with broken or open shells.

2 Bring water to the boil. Add mussels. Cover and steam for 3 to 5 minutes or until they open. Remove mussels from shells, discarding any that do not open. Place in a bowl. Cover and set aside.

3 Cover snow peas with boiling water. Leave for 1 minute. Drain and cool under cold running water. Add snow peas to mussels.

4 Halve lychees, removing stones. Mix with mussels. Sprinkle over ginger.

5 Pour dressing over mussel mixture. Toss to coat all ingredients. Chill, covered, for 30 minutes. Drain off any excess dressing. Serve on individual plates.

SERVES 6

HERBED GREEN BEANS

¼ pound butter or margarine

1 teaspoon chopped fresh parsley

1 teaspoon chopped chives

½ teaspoon chopped fresh basil

1 pound green beans

1 small onion, chopped

1 clove garlic, chopped

freshly ground black pepper, to taste

¼ cup sunflower seeds, to serve

fresh chives, to garnish

1 Combine butter with parsley, chives, marjoram and basil. Set aside. Trim beans if desired, and place them in a saucepan with the onion and garlic.

2 Cover with boiling water. Cook until tender. Drain well.

3 Add herb butter to the pan with beans, swirling around briefly until beans are well coated.

4 Season to taste. Add sunflower seeds just before serving. Tie beans into bundles with chives if liked before serving.

SERVES 6

TOMATO DRESSING

1 cup tomato juice

juice 1 lime or ½ lemon

2 scallions, finely chopped

2 cloves garlic, chopped

Worcestershire sauce, to taste

Tabasco sauce, to taste

freshly ground black pepper

Combine all ingredients thoroughly. Store in an airtight container in the refrigerator. Use as directed.

MAKES 1 CUP

❤ **EASY ACCOMPANIMENT**

Peas and beans are delicious if tossed in butter once cooked and drained.

ROSY DHAL

1 pound yellow lentils

3 tablespoons oil

2 to 3 onions, finely sliced

2 to 3 tomatoes, skinned and chopped

2 teaspoons turmeric

1 teaspoon cayenne

3 tablespoons tomato paste

1 Soak lentils in enough water to cover for 30 minutes. Sauté onion in oil until soft.

2 Add tomatoes, turmeric and cayenne. Cook, stirring for 5 minutes.

3 Bring lentils to the boil. Stir in onion mixture. Lower heat. Simmer 1 hour. Stir in tomato paste.

MAKES ABOUT 3 CUPS

LONG BEAN SALAD

1 pound long (green) beans

5 tablespoons olive or walnut oil

8 scallions, finely chopped

3 tablespoons snipped fresh dill

1 tablespoon tarragon vinegar

2 red pimientos, diced

1 to 3 tablespoons pine nuts

1 Trim beans. Slice into four. Almost cover with boiling water. Boil briskly for 3 to 5 minutes.

2 Refresh quickly under cold running water, drain and place into salad bowl.

3 Sprinkle with oil. Toss well to coat beans. Add scallions and dill. Sprinkle with vinegar. Toss again and refrigerate for at least 30 minutes.

4 Add pimientos and pine nuts. Toss once more and serve.

SERVES 6

BRAISED BROAD BEANS

2 pounds broad beans

5 tablespoons oil

1 onion, chopped

1 clove garlic, crushed

1 cup water mixed with 1 tablespoon tomato purée

1½ tablespoons chopped fresh parsley

1½ tablespoons chopped fresh dill

freshly ground black pepper, to taste

pinch nutmeg

1 Shell beans. Heat the oil in a saucepan. Add the beans, onion and garlic. Cook over moderate heat, stirring, for 2 minutes. Add the remaining ingredients and bring to the boil.

2 Cover the pan. Cook for 25 minutes, adding more water if necessary.

SERVES 6

ROSY DHAL

Pulse foods are eaten throughout India and Asia and contain the highest protein values known. There are innumerable recipes for dhal but this is a favorite. This delicious vegetable dish can be served with any meal but it is, of course, best served with curry and rice. It is also delicious when used as a vegetable stuffing.

Braised Broad Beans

SOAKING PULSES

When soaking dried beans, cover with hot water to speed up the process by softening the outer coat.

STRINGING BEANS

Stringing peas and beans is easy. Simply cut partially through the stem end, leaving the stem attached at one end. Pull off the string along the pod. Repeat at the tip to string the other side if necessary.

CALAMARI WITH SNOW PEAS

1 pound prepared calamari hoods

½ pound snow peas, trimmed

⅓ cup stock

1 teaspoon soy sauce

½ teaspoon sugar

1 slice fresh ginger root, finely chopped

3 tablespoons oil

½ cup sliced bamboo shoots

2 scallions, cut into ¾-inch lengths

1 teaspoon cornstarch

2 teaspoons water

1 Cut calamari hoods into 1-inch squares. Blanch snow peas. Combine stock, soy sauce and sugar. Set aside.

2 Stir-fry the calamari and ginger in oil for about 1 minute. Add bamboo shoots and scallions. Stir-fry for another 30 seconds.

3 Blend in the stock mixture. Bring to the boil, adding the snow peas just to heat through.

4 Thicken by stirring in cornstarch blended first in a bit of cold water. Bring to the boil. Serve on individual dishes or in scallop shells.

SERVES 4 TO 6

BEAN AND PEA SOUP

¼ cup kidney beans

¼ cup lima beans

¼ cup yellow split peas

¼ cup chick peas

7 cups chicken stock

1 bay leaf

1 onion, chopped

½ cup chopped red pepper

¼ cup chopped celery

¼ cup chopped carrots

1 tablespoon chopped parsley

1 clove garlic, crushed

3 tablespoons oil

4½ cups beef stock

1 bay leaf

pinch marjoram

pinch basil

½ cup tomatoes, peeled, seeded and chopped

1 Soak beans and peas overnight in chicken stock. Add bay leaf. Bring to boil. Simmer over low heat for 1 hour or until tender.

2 Cook onion, pepper, celery, carrots, parsley and garlic in oil for 5 minutes. Pour in beef stock and bay leaf. Simmer until all vegetables are tender.

3 Add beans and peas and all remaining ingredients. Simmer for 20 minutes. Remove bay leaves before serving.

SERVES 6 TO 8

FETTUCCINE WITH SHRIMP AND PEAS

1 pound cooked fettuccine, drained and kept warm

1 scallion, chopped

1 pound cooked shrimp, peeled and deveined

1 cup cooked peas

8 snow peas, blanched

SAUCE

2 egg yolks

1½ tablespoons white wine vinegar

½ tablespoon fresh lemon juice

½ tablespoon finely chopped ginger root

finely ground black pepper

1½ tablespoons hot water

⅓ cup olive oil

1½ tablespoons sesame oil

¼ cup heavy cream

1 In bowl, combine fettuccine, scallion, shrimp and peas. Keep warm.

2 TO PREPARE SAUCE: Combine egg yolks, vinegar, lemon juice, ginger and seasoning in a food processor. Process 30 seconds. Add hot water and oils in thin stream. Add cream in thin stream. Process until combined.

3 Toss sauce through fettuccine. Serve hot, garnished with snow peas.

SERVES 4

bread crumbs, and sprinkle half over the top of the pastry. Spread the vegetables in one layer. Sprinkle with the remaining cheese and crumbs. Season with basil and pepper.

5 Roll up the pastry. Seal and brush with melted butter. Bake in a moderately hot oven 375°F for 35 minutes. Before serving, decorate with chervil and carrot straws.

SERVES 6

Vegetable Strudel

VEGETABLE STRUDEL

2 carrots, thinly sliced

½ pound green beans, trimmed and sliced

½ pound broccoli florets

1 leek

2 tablespoons butter or margarine

4 mushroom caps, sliced

1 stick celery, finely chopped

¼ pound bean sprouts

5 sheets filo pastry

4 tablespoons butter or margarine, melted

1 cup grated Cheddar cheese

1 cup fresh bread crumbs

1½ tablespoons finely chopped fresh basil

freshly ground pepper, to taste

fresh chervil, to garnish

carrot, cut in straws, to garnish

1 Blanch the carrots, beans and broccoli individually, drain and set aside.

2 Wash the leek well. Slice the white part very finely. Melt the butter and cook the leek over low heat until it is soft. Add the mushrooms to the pan. Cook for 1 minute.

3 Add the celery, then stir in the bean sprouts and the remaining prepared vegetables. Toss well. Allow to cool.

4 Brush each sheet of filo pastry with melted butter. Place them one on top of the other. Mix together the cheese and

Sweet Corn

Nothing is more delicious than fresh corn, steamed and served with butter and a little salt to taste if required. In fact, the fresher the corn, the sweeter it is. That is because the sugar in corn converts to starch on aging. To use fresh corn in recipes, remove corn from cob with a sharp knife, cutting the kernels as close as possible to the cob. There's no waste with baby corn. It can be eaten whole and is perfect lightly steamed or in stir-fries. The husk of sweet corn makes a natural cooking vessel. First peel back the husk and remove the silky threads. Then replace and tie the husks loosely with string to hold in place over the cob.

MEXICAN SUCCOTASH

1 cup fresh corn kernels
½ red pepper, cut into large dice
½ green pepper, cut into large dice
4 small white onions, halved
½ cup peas
½ cup fresh lima beans
1 tablespoon oil
1 tablespoon chopped fresh basil
fresh basil or parsley, to garnish

1 Place all the vegetables in a steamer and cook for 10 minutes.
2 Heat oil in a pan. Add vegetables. Sauté vegetables for several minutes. Add basil. Serve with fresh herbs.

SERVES 2

MEXICAN CORN ON THE COB

4 hard-boiled eggs
4 tablespoons butter or margarine, softened
4 tablespoons heavy cream
½ teaspoon Tabasco sauce
3 tablespoons chopped parsley
freshly ground black pepper, to taste
4 ears fresh corn
1 tablespoon sugar

1 Mash eggs with fork till smooth. Blend in butter, cream, Tabasco, parsley and seasoning.
2 Cut each ear into three pieces. Cook in boiling water with sugar for 4 to 10 minutes or until tender. Drain.
3 Serve hot, topped with egg and butter mixture.

SERVES 4

SWEET CORN STRUDEL

*Canned or frozen corn kernels are equally
delicious in this strudel.*

2 cups cooked corn, cooled

1 egg, beaten

1 sheet ready-made flaky pastry

1 Mix egg with corn.
2 Spread corn mixture evenly over sheet of
flaky pastry stopping ½ inch from all edges.
3 Roll up tightly taking care not to break
the pastry. Brush end seam with a little extra
egg to seal.
4 Place carefully on a flat baking tray.
Bake in a 450°F oven for 20 to 25 minutes
or until golden.

SERVES 4

CORN AND POTATO PUFFS

1 large canned corn, drained

**4 medium potatoes, cooked and dry
mashed**

1 red pepper, finely diced

4 scallions, finely diced

3 tablespoons flour

3 tablespoons chutney

2 tablespoons plain yogurt

1 egg, beaten

2 cloves garlic, crushed

oil for deep-frying

1 In a bowl, combine drained corn with
potato, red pepper, scallions, flour, chutney,
yogurt, egg and garlic.
2 Heat oil in a pan. Fry spoonfuls of the
mixture until golden. Drain on absorbent
paper. Serve as a snack or a side dish.

SERVES 4 TO 6

ROOT CROPS

Potatoes are probably the most well-known of all vegetables. Choose potatoes that are firm and smooth with no blemishes or green skin.

Sweet potatoes can be used in many of the same dishes. Choose sweet potatoes with unblemished, uniformly colored, smooth skin and no soft or moist spots. Avoid any that are sprouting.

Carrots are sweet, crisp and firm when young, but as they age become limp and develop woody cores. Look for bright orange carrots and avoid any that look dry or split. Scrub and remove root ends before using cooked or raw.

Ivory parsnips have a starchy flesh and a fruity smell. Look for medium-sized, unblemished parsnips with smooth, firm flesh.

Turnips have a white, crisp flesh with a sweet to hot flavor. Choose small to medium-sized unblemished turnips with no moist spots. Look for bright, fresh tops — which, incidentally, may be used in salads. Wash and peel before baking, steaming or puréeing. Rutabagas are equally delicious.

Beets make wonderful salads and soups. Try whole baby beets or grate raw beets over coleslaw.

POTATO PATTIES

2 pounds potatoes, peeled

2 tablespoons butter or margarine

2 eggs, beaten

2 to 3 tablespoons flour

1 cup mushroom stock, including mushrooms (see Note)

½ cup bread crumbs

1 tablespoon sour cream

1 Cook potatoes until tender. Drain well. Mash potatoes with half the butter and most of the egg until thoroughly blended. If mixture is too liquid to hold its shape, add a little flour. Beat in well.

2 Place potato dough on a floured board. Work it into a thick rectangle. Roll out into a piece about 10 to 12 inches long. Cut into circles with a biscuit cutter. Top each with a few mushrooms. Fold over to form a crescent and press edge together. Brush with remainder of egg. Coat with bread crumbs.

3 Melt rest of butter in a pan and fry patties carefully on high heat. Cook a few at a time, to avoid burning.

4 Brown patties on each side, 3 to 5 minutes, turning carefully with a spatula. Drain on absorbent paper, and place on a serving dish. Add mushroom stock to sour cream. Blend well. Serve sauce separately in a sauce boat.

NOTE: To prepare mushroom stock, add 2 ounces dried mushrooms to 1 quart of water in a large saucepan. Soak for 4 to 8 hours. Bring to the boil. Simmer for 5 to 8 minutes or until mushrooms are tender. Remove mushrooms. Drain and chop. Use in sauces or fillings. Strain stock. Freeze or refrigerate for several days.

SERVES 6 TO 8

SCALLOPED SWEET POTATOES

The faintly scented flesh of the sweet potato has a taste that will grow on you. Sir Francis Drake, who took it to England, thought it more delicious than the sweetest apple.

1½ pounds sweet potatoes, peeled and thinly sliced

2 cups milk

3 tablespoons flour

2 slices bacon, cooked and diced

1 cup grated tasty cheese

½ cup scallions, finely cut

chopped fresh parsley

freshly ground black pepper

nutmeg and paprika

1 Arrange sweet potatoes in a shallow, greased casserole dish. Whisk together milk, flour, bacon, cheese, scallions, parsley and seasoning. Pour over sweet potatoes.

2 Bake in a moderate oven 350°F for 45 minutes or until sweet potatoes are tender. Sprinkle with nutmeg and paprika to garnish. Serve as a side dish or as a main meal.

SERVES 6

SPANISH OMELET

3 tablespoons olive oil

1 large potato, peeled and diced

1 large red onion, finely chopped

5 eggs

freshly ground black pepper, to taste

1 Heat the oil in a large skillet. Sauté the potato and onion slowly, stirring occasionally, until both are cooked but not brown.

2 Whisk the eggs with pepper. Pour into the pan with vegetables, spreading evenly. Cover the pan. Lower the heat and allow the omelet to cook for about 10 minutes.

3 Place a plate of similar size to your frying pan over the top of it. Invert the omelet. Return it immediately to the pan. Allow the other side to brown. It will be thick and golden in color when it is ready. Serve in wedges with salad.

SERVES 4

DILL-MUSTARD POTATO SALAD

2 quarts chicken stock

2 pounds tiny new potatoes

¾ cup vegetable oil

1 egg, room temperature

3 tablespoons Dijon mustard

3 tablespoons finely chopped fresh dill or 2 teaspoons dried dill

1 teaspoon red wine vinegar

1 teaspoon lemon juice

freshly ground black pepper, to taste

½ cup sour cream

3 celery stalks, stringed and thinly sliced

1 onion, thinly sliced

½ bunch chives, snipped

1 Wash potatoes but do not peel. Combine stock and potatoes in a large pan. Bring to boil over high heat. Reduce heat. Simmer potatoes until just tender. Rinse with cold water to cool, and drain well.

2 In a food processor or blender combine 3 tablespoons oil with egg, mustard, dill, vinegar, lemon juice and pepper. Process until mixture is slightly thickened, about 10 seconds.

3 With machine running, slowly pour remaining oil through feed tube in thin, steady stream. Mix well. Add sour cream. Blend 3 seconds to combine.

4 Slice potatoes into quarters. Combine in a salad bowl with celery and onion. Pour over

the dressing. Fold through the salad. Cover and refrigerate until ready to serve. Garnish with chives.

SERVES 6

Dill-Mustard Potato Salad

 CRISP CHIPS

When making chips, ensure the potato sticks are well dried before immersing in hot oil. Never fill the pan more than two-thirds with oil, to prevent boiling over.

Step-by-Step Techniques

PIROSHKI

Yeast Pastry

1 package yeast

2¾ cups warm milk

2 pounds sifted flour

7 tablespoons butter or margarine, melted

4 eggs, lightly beaten

4 tablespoons sugar

1 teaspoon salt

Filling

2 pounds potatoes, peeled

4 tablespoons butter or margarine

oil for deep frying

1 To Prepare Yeast Pastry: In a large mixing bowl, mix yeast and warm milk. Add half the flour. Mix with a wooden spoon. Cover and set aside for 1 hour until batter has risen about double in size.

2 Add butter, eggs, sugar and salt. Mix well with a wooden spoon. Fold in remaining flour. Knead well until the dough forms a ball and leaves the sides of the bowl.

3 Cover and set aside for 2 hours — again it should double in size.

4 Knead dough well on a lightly floured board for 3 to 4 minutes. Cover and set aside for 1 hour.

5 To Prepare Filling: Cook potatoes until tender. Mash with butter. Beat till very smooth.

6 To Make Piroshki: Roll the yeast pastry out to about ½-inch thick on a floured board. Cut out circles with a biscuit cutter. Set aside to rise a little.

7 Gather scraps of leftover pastry. Roll into a ball, roll out again and cut into circles and let rise.

8 Place a large tablespoon of filling in each circle. Flatten filling with the back of the

To prepare Yeast Pastry, add half flour to yeast mixture with wooden spoon and allow to rise.

Add butter, eggs, sugar and salt and fold in remaining flour.

Knead well until dough forms a ball.

spoon. Fold pastry over the filling. Pinch the edges to seal. Place seam side down on a floured board. Cover and set aside to rise for 10 to 15 minutes.

9 Heat oil in a large saucepan. Do not fill more than three-quarters. Place one piroshki into oil. If it is at the right temperature, the fat should bubble and the pastry will brown in 1 minute or less. Turn.

10 When temperature is correct, place up to six piroshki in oil. It is difficult to control

more than that number. When each is cooked, place on absorbent paper to drain. Allow to cool. Serve as a main course or a snack.

FILLING VARIATION 1

1 pound cooked green beans

2 sliced onions

2 tablespoons oil

4 sprigs fresh dill, finely chopped

freshly ground black pepper, to taste

Sauté beans and onions in oil, stirring constantly. Turn heat off. Add dill and pepper. Mix well.

FILLING VARIATION 2

2 pounds sliced mushrooms

4 tablespoons butter or margarine

1 chopped onion

¼ cup sour cream

Cook mushrooms in half the butter until tender. Remove from pan. Sauté onion in remaining butter. Blend in sour cream and mushrooms. Simmer for 10 to 15 minutes.

MAKES ABOUT 35 TO 40 PIROSHKI

Piroshki with Mushroom Filling

 PEELING

Peel root vegetables with a vegetable peeler or a small sharp knife if thicker peeling is required. Peel can be used to make a vegetable stock.

*Marinated Fish
with Carrots*

MIREPOIX

*Carrots are one of the
basic ingredients used to
flavor stock and to make
a mirepoix, an aromatic
base for many dishes.
Other ingredients are
onion, celery and herbs.*

MARINATED FISH
WITH CARROTS

**2 pounds bass, cod or other similar fish
fillets**

3 tablespoons flour

4 tablespoons butter or margarine

**1 pound carrots, peeled and
julienned**

3 large onions, sliced

1 tablespoon flour, extra

**2 pounds tomatoes, peeled and finely
chopped**

1 Bring carrots to the boil in a small
amount of water. Simmer for 15 minutes.
Remove carrots. Reserve cooking liquid.

2 Cut fish into pieces about 2 inches square.
Dust each piece in flour.

3 Heat 2 tablespoons butter in a skillet.
Add the fish pieces, skin side down. Cook
for 3 minutes, then turn and cook for
another 2 minutes.

4 Sauté onions in remaining butter until
cooked but not brown. Sprinkle extra flour
over onions. Blend in tomatoes with juice,
stirring constantly. Mix in 1 cup of reserved
carrot cooking liquid.

5 Place carrots in the bottom of a covered
frying pan. Place fish pieces on top. Pour
over tomato and onion mixture.

6 Simmer, covered, for 10 minutes.
Serve hot or cold.

SERVES 4 TO 6

POTATO STICKS

½ pound potatoes

2 egg yolks

4 tablespoons butter or margarine

1¼ cups sifted flour

freshly ground black pepper, to taste

1 tablespoon chopped chives

1 egg, beaten

1 Peel potatoes and cook in boiling water until tender. Drain well. Mash with the egg yolks and butter until creamy.

2 Add the flour, pepper and chives. Mix well. Form the dough into a round shape. Refrigerate for 30 minutes.

3 Roll dough out into a rectangle ½ inch thick. Cut into sticks ½ inch wide and 3 inches long. Twist and brush lightly with some beaten egg.

4 Place on a greased baking tray. Bake in a 400°F oven for 10 minutes or until golden brown and crisp. Leave potato sticks on the tray until they are cool. Serve as a snack or part of a meal.

MAKES 40

SWEDISH HASSELBACK POTATOES

12 potatoes

1 teaspoon salt

4 tablespoons butter or margarine

4 tablespoons grated Parmesan cheese

3 tablespoons bread crumbs

1 Peel potatoes and cut into thin slices not quite through to the lower edge, so that the slices hold together.

2 Place potatoes, with slices up, into a well buttered casserole dish. Sprinkle with salt and dot with butter. Bake in a 450°F oven for 20 minutes, basting occasionally with the melted butter.

3 Sprinkle with cheese and bread crumbs. Bake for another 25 minutes without basting. This goes very well with roast meats.

SERVES 6

WARM BEET SALAD

2 pounds large beets

7 tablespoons olive oil

1 tablespoon white wine vinegar

freshly ground black pepper, to taste

1 tablespoon fennel, grated

1 large onion, sliced

2 tablespoons butter or margarine

chives, to garnish

1 Trim beets and wrap each in foil. Bake in a 350°F oven for an hour or until they are tender when tested with a toothpick. Peel while still warm.

2 Cut beets into strips. Whisk together oil, vinegar and pepper. Pour over the beets. You may not need all of it. Sprinkle with fennel.

3 Sauté the onion in butter until it is tender and golden. Pour over beets and mix gently. Garnish with chives.

SERVES 6 TO 8

AVOID GREEN POTATOES

Never use potatoes with green patches on their skin as they can be toxic. Do not store in plastic bags as this can cause greening — these potatoes should never be eaten. Do not refrigerate potatoes.

JACKET POTATOES

To prevent the skin of baked, boiled or steamed potatoes from bursting, prick with a fork before cooking.

GLAZED CARROTS

A simple glaze for cooked carrots is a little melted butter combined with some brown sugar and chives. Toss the carrots in this mixture and serve.

CREAMY POTATOES

Cream potatoes with sour cream, butter and chives for a delicious change.

STUFFED POTATOES

A delicious recipe for the microwave oven.

4 large potatoes

1 large onion, sliced

½ cup frozen or fresh peas

½ cup green pepper, chopped

½ cup sweet corn kernels

½ cup plain yogurt

3 tablespoons pine nuts

3 tablespoons sunflower seeds (optional)

1 teaspoon soy sauce

1 to 2 cups grated tasty cheese

1 Wash and prick the potatoes. Cook at 100% for about 12 to 16 minutes, or until just soft. Cover. Leave to stand while you prepare the filling.

2 Cook the onion with remaining vegetables at 100% for 4 to 5 minutes, covered tightly with plastic wrap.

3 Slice the tops off the potatoes. Scoop out the centers, leaving about a ½-inch thickness of potato inside the skins.

4 Chop the scooped potato and the lids. Mix with the yogurt, seeds and the onion and vegetable mixture. Blend in soy sauce.

5 Pile the mixture back into the skins. Sprinkle with grated cheese. Return to the microwave and cook at 100% for 3 to 6 minutes or until heated through. When the cheese has thoroughly melted, the potatoes should be done.

FILLING VARIATIONS

- Onion, corn, tomatoes, pistachio nuts.
- Onion, mushrooms, tomatoes, grated Parmesan cheese, fresh or dried basil.
- Onion, shredded fish, shrimp, tomato paste, parsley.
- Onion, chicken or ham, mushrooms, yogurt, parsley.

COOKING POTATOES

Prepare potatoes as close to cooking as possible. Once peeled, potatoes begin to discolor due to oxidation. To prevent this, wrap in plastic wrap. Covering with water also prevents discoloration, but this is not recommended due to loss of nutrients.

- Onion, toasted coconut, saffron, chopped almonds, peas.
- Onion, corn, cooked mixed beans, tomato paste.

SERVES 4

BRAISED PARSNIPS WITH CHOPPED EGGS AND TOMATOES

For a more substantial dish, add extra chopped eggs, and sprinkle with grated cheese.

1 pound parsnips, peeled and sliced

6 tablespoons butter or margarine

1 medium-sized onion, chopped

1 clove garlic, crushed

2 tomatoes, skinned, seeded and chopped (see Note)

freshly ground pepper, to taste

2 hard-boiled eggs, chopped

1 tablespoon chopped parsley

1 Boil parsnips in just enough water to cover for 15 minutes. Drain well.

2 Melt butter in a frying pan. Sauté onion and garlic until tender but not colored. Add tomatoes, parsnips and seasoning.

3 Transfer mixture to a shallow ovenproof dish. Bake in a 400°F oven for 20 minutes. Serve sprinkled with chopped egg and parsley.

NOTE: Pierce tomatoes several times with a sharp knife. Drop into hot water for 1 minute. Skin will peel off easily. Cut in half and gently squeeze out seeds. Chopped tomato pulp is known as *tomates concassee*. Tomatoes are now ready to use as required.

SERVES 4

ROSEMARY LAMB COOKED ON A BED OF POTATOES

This is a favorite way of serving a leg of lamb. The vegetable bed collects all the lovely juices from the lamb, as well as flavoring the leg and keeping it moist. It is important though to use a very lean leg of lamb or remove most of the fat. New Zealand lamb or genuine spring lamb would be perfect for this dish.

3 to 4 pound leg lamb

2 cloves garlic

3 tablespoons fresh rosemary sprigs

salt and freshly ground black pepper, to taste

3 tablespoons olive oil

3 leeks, sliced and washed

2 pounds potatoes, peeled and thinly sliced

1½ cups beef stock

1 Remove any surplus fat from leg of lamb. Peel garlic and cut into slivers. Season surface of lamb with salt and pepper.

2 With a sharp knife, make small incisions under the skin of the lamb. Insert a sliver of garlic and a small sprig of rosemary into each.

3 Heat oil in a heavy roasting pan. Sauté leeks until soft and translucent. Add potatoes to the leeks in the pan. Mix through remaining sprigs of rosemary. Pour over stock.

4 Place lamb on vegetable bed. Roast in a 375°F oven for 20 minutes. Lower heat to 300°F and cook another 40 minutes or so for pink lamb, 1 hour for a medium. Serve sliced thickly with the vegetables and a seasonal green vegetable, lightly steamed.

NOTE: Allow 20 to 25 minutes cooking time per pound.

SERVES 4 TO 6

Rosemary Lamb Cooked on a Bed of Potatoes

PARSNIPS WITH HERBS

6 parsnips

6 tablespoons butter or margarine

juice 1 lemon

freshly ground black pepper to taste

1 cup chicken stock

1 tablespoon finely chopped fresh herbs (parsley, chives, dill, marjoram)

fresh thyme, for decoration

1 Peel parsnips and cut into large matchsticks. Place the butter, lemon juice, pepper and stock into a frying pan. Bring to the boil.

2 Add the parsnips and herbs. Cook, uncovered, until the stock has reduced and the parsnips are tender. Add more stock if necessary. Garnish with thyme.

SERVES 4

 ROAST VEGETABLES

Carrots, parsnips and turnips make delicious roast vegetables.

Radishes with Sour Cream

RADISHES WITH SOUR CREAM

15 to 20 small round radishes, washed and thinly sliced

1 hard-boiled egg, chopped (see Note)

¼ cup sour cream

sprigs fresh dill

Combine radish slices with egg and sour cream. Mix well. Arrange and serve garnished with dill.

NOTE: To cook a hard-boiled egg, place egg into cold water and bring to the boil. Simmer for 8 minutes. Cool under cold, running water. Peel and use as directed.

SERVES 4

 RADISHES

Radishes can also be a useful ingredient in quick and easy summery stir-fries.

BAKED TURNIPS

2 turnips, peeled and diced

½ cup chicken stock

4 tablespoons dark honey

Place turnips in a buttered casserole dish. Mix warm stock with honey. Pour over turnips. Cover the dish. Bake in a 350° F oven for 45 minutes or until tender.

SERVES 4

BABY CARROTS WITH FRESH BASIL

1 pound baby (very young) carrots

3 tablespoons finely chopped fresh basil

6 tablespoons butter or margarine

1 Place carrots in a saucepan with enough boiling water to cover. Bring to the boil and cook for 5 minutes.

2 Drain, toss well with basil and butter over a gentle heat. Allow the butter to melt, mixing well with the carrots.

SERVES 6

CARROT AND CHIVE SALAD

4 carrots, scrubbed and grated

2 bunches chives, snipped

½ bunch scallions, slivered

½ cup golden raisins

HERB VINAIGRETTE

1 tablespoon Dijon mustard

1½ tablespoons white wine vinegar

1½ tablespoons chopped fresh herbs, e.g., parsley, chives or thyme

⅓ cup olive oil

freshly ground black pepper

1 Combine carrots with chives, scallions and raisins in a bowl.

2 TO PREPARE VINAIGRETTE: Place mustard in a bowl. Whisk in vinegar and herbs. Gradually whisk in oil until mixture thickens. Season to taste.

3 Pour vinaigrette over salad.

SERVES 4

GADO-GADO

2 large carrots, thinly sliced

½ pound green beans, trimmed

½ pound bean sprouts

1 cup shredded cabbage

1 large onion, chopped

1 cucumber, sliced thinly

3 hard-boiled eggs

3 tablespoons chopped scallions, to garnish

SAUCE

1 cup unsalted roasted peanuts

⅓ cup sugar

3 cloves garlic, peeled

3 tablespoons lemon juice or vinegar

1 Blanch carrots for 2 minutes. Drain. Slice beans diagonally. Blanch 2 minutes. Drain. Blanch bean sprouts, cabbage and onion for 1 minute. Drain well.

2 Toss vegetables together. Arrange on a platter with cucumber and sliced eggs. Set aside.

3 Combine all sauce ingredients. Process in a food processor until mixture is thick and smooth.

4 Drizzle sauce over vegetables. Garnish with scallions.

SERVES 6

LEFTOVER POTATOES

Use leftover mashed potatoes to make croquettes, pie toppings or use it as a base for 'bubble and squeak'.

MICROWAVE POTATOES

Microwave potatoes by first scrubbing well with a brush and pricking in several places with a fork. Arrange in a circular pattern on the turntable. Cook, uncovered, at 100% for 5 to 7 minutes for one; 7 to 9 minutes for two; 9 to 11 minutes for three; and 11 to 13 minutes for four. Stand for 5 minutes before serving.

MUSHROOMS

Mushrooms seem to lend themselves to just about anything creative in the kitchen. Their flavor is unmistakable in salads, soups, stews, sauces, stir-fries, pies, meat loaves and breads. Available year round, mushrooms come as buttons, cups and flats. Never buy any that are slimy or dry in appearance or store them in plastic bags. Instead, refrigerate mushrooms in paper or cloth bags and they will keep for a week. Preparation couldn't be easier, and there's no waste whatsoever. Simply wipe over with a damp cloth and use whole or cut into quarters, halves or slices.

GRILLED MUSHROOM CAPS

1 pound medium-sized mushroom caps
2 to 4 cloves garlic, crushed
4 tablespoons butter or margarine
5 tablespoons bread crumbs
3 tablespoons grated Parmesan cheese
4 bacon slices, chopped

1 Wipe mushrooms. Carefully remove the stalks. Chop the stalks finely. Mix with the crushed garlic.

2 Mash the butter with a fork. Mix in the bread crumbs, cheese and the mushroom stalks. Fry or broil the bacon until crisp. Drain on absorbent paper. Add to the cheese mixture.

3 Fill the mushroom caps with the mixture. Place under a hot broiler to brown quickly. Serve as a snack or a side dish.

SERVES 4 TO 6

CHICKEN AND MUSHROOM PIE

3 pound chicken

3 tablespoons dry sherry

6 black peppercorns

½ tablespoon chopped fresh herbs

¼ teaspoon sage

1 leek, sliced

1 onion, chopped

1 clove garlic, crushed

4 tablespoons butter

½ pound fresh mushrooms, sliced

freshly ground pepper

12 sheets filo pastry

6 tablespoons butter, melted

1 tablespoon sesame seeds

1 Clean and rinse chicken. Place in large saucepan with sherry, peppercorns and herbs. Cover with cold water and bring to boil. Simmer for 45 minutes. Allow to cool in liquid then drain, discarding stock.

2 Remove skin and bones from chicken and discard. Cut up chicken meat and set aside.

3 Sauté leek, onion and garlic in butter until transparent. Add mushrooms and pepper and cook 2 minutes. Add mushroom mixture to chicken meat, stirring to blend. Place chicken mixture in an 8-inch pie tin.

4 Cut pastry sheets in half and keep covered with plastic wrap or damp cloth while preparing the pie top. Layer pastry over filling, brushing every second sheet with butter. Roughly tuck pastry around edge of dish. Brush with butter and sprinkle with sesame seeds.

5 Bake on the top rack of a 400°F oven for 45 minutes or until golden brown. Serve hot.

SERVES 6 TO 8

Grilled Mushroom Caps

PORK AND MUSHROOMS WITH GINGER MANGO DRESSING

1 head lettuce, leaves washed and dried

1½ pound pork fillet, baked and sliced into thin medallions

4 stalks celery, sliced

1 mango, seeded, peeled and sliced

1 red apple, sliced and sprinkled with lemon juice to prevent browning

½ pineapple, peeled and chopped

¼ pound mushrooms – chantarelles are appropriate for this dish

1 cup hazelnuts, toasted

chives

freshly ground black pepper, to taste

GINGER MANGO DRESSING

2 mangoes, peeled and sliced

⅔ cup light mayonnaise

1 teaspoon minced ginger

1 Line salad bowl with a few large lettuce leaves. Tear the remaining leaves into bite-sized pieces and mix with the rest of the salad ingredients except for chives and pepper.

2 TO PREPARE DRESSING: Purée mango, mayonnaise and ginger until smooth.

3 Toss salad ingredients lightly with dressing and arrange in salad bowl. Top with chopped chives and a twist of freshly ground black pepper. Serve as a main meal.

SERVES 4 TO 6

SHERRIED MUSHROOM SOUP

2 tablespoons butter or margarine

½ pound mushrooms, finely chopped

2 cans concentrated mushroom soup

1¾ cups milk

3 tablespoons cream

3 tablespoons sherry

freshly ground black pepper, to taste

1 tablespoon sour cream

**croutons and chopped chives
for serving**

1 Melt butter in pan. Cook mushrooms for 4 minutes until tender. Pour in soup, stirring lightly.

2 Gradually add milk, stirring until soup is smooth, with a developed flavor. Add cream, sherry and seasonings.

3 Serve in warmed soup bowls. Garnish with sour cream, croutons and a sprinkling of chopped chives.

SERVES 4

TARRAGON MUSHROOMS À LA GRECQUE

1 pound button mushrooms

3 tablespoons chopped fresh parsley

**3 tablespoons chopped fresh tarragon
or 1 tablespoon dried tarragon**

2 cloves garlic, crushed with a pinch salt

juice 1 lemon

1 tomato, peeled, seeded and chopped

1 cup water

¼ cup olive oil

1 bay leaf

freshly ground black pepper, to taste

1 Wipe mushrooms and trim stalks. Place in heavy-based saucepan with parsley, tarragon, garlic and lemon juice.

2 Add tomatoes to the pan with remaining ingredients. Bring to the boil. Cover and simmer gently for 8 minutes. Serve hot or chilled, with crusty bread or as an accompaniment to broiled or barbecued meats.

SERVES 4 AS A SIDE DISH

STUFFED MUSHROOMS

16 mushroom caps

FILLING

½ cup fresh white bread crumbs

½ cup finely grated Parmesan cheese

1 cup chopped ham

3 tablespoons capers, finely chopped

**½ cup grated cheese, Emmenthaler
or Gruyère**

1 clove garlic, crushed

¼ cup finely chopped parsley

freshly ground black pepper

lemon juice

3 tablespoons olive oil

GARNISH

8 slices smoked ham

6 lettuce leaves

1 tablespoon lemon juice

1 Carefully remove stalks from mushrooms. Chop stalks finely. Blend with filling ingredients except for seasoning, lemon juice and oil.

2 Arrange mushroom caps in a buttered ovenproof dish. Season with a twist of pepper and a squeeze of lemon juice.

3 Spoon filling evenly into caps, shaping a little. Sprinkle with olive oil. Bake in a 400°F oven for 8 minutes.

4 TO PREPARE GARNISH: Cut ham into circles with a biscuit cutter. Heat lettuce with lemon juice very gently in a covered saucepan until it has wilted.

5 Place a ham circle under each mushroom cap and serve on the bed of lettuce.

SERVES 8

 CROUTONS

Prepare croutons by frying cubed bread in equal quantities of butter and oil until golden. Drain well.

LEAFY CROPS

Nature's bounty when it comes to leafy vegetables seems endless.
Today there are many varieties of lettuce to choose from.
And all will add color, flavor and texture to salads.

Cabbage is one of the oldest known vegetables and comes in several
varieties. Choose cabbages with crisp, compact, bright, unblemished
leaves. They should be heavy for their size. Wash each leaf well
before using and remove hard center ribs. Brussels sprouts are closely
related to the cabbage. Choose small, firm, brightly colored sprouts.
Trim ends, remove outer leaves and rinse well before cooking.

Both spinach and Swiss chard can be used cooked or raw, and should
be stored in plastic bags in the refrigerator. Wash leaves well before
using and remove leaf from thick center stalk of the chard. When
choosing spinach look for crisp, tender, unblemished leaves.
Swiss chard should be glossy with white or red stems.

Witloof or Belgian endive comes as a head of small, smooth,
white leaves with a bitter flavor. They should be trimmed,
cored, and washed before using raw or cooked.

Chicken Soufflé Roll

1 Grease and line a jelly roll pan with wax paper. Gently cook spinach in butter in a covered pan for 5 to 6 minutes until it wilts. Cool slightly. Chop roughly. Purée the spinach in a food processor with egg yolks.

2 Beat egg whites until stiff and fold into the mixture. Spread over the prepared tray. Sprinkle with Parmesan cheese. Bake in a 400°F oven for about 12 minutes or until firm to touch.

3 **To Prepare Filling:** Gently sweat mushrooms and onion in butter until tender. Add flour. Cook for 1 minute without browning. Gradually blend in milk. Bring to the boil, stirring constantly, then simmer for 3 minutes.

4 Add chicken, cream cheese and sour cream. Cook until cheese melts. Blend in mustard and seasoning.

5 Turn spinach soufflé onto a soft dish towel. Remove paper. Spread cooled filling over soufflé. Roll up from the longest side with the aid of the towel. Serve sliced with salad.

SERVES 6 TO 8

COOKING SPINACH

Spinach shouldn't be cooked with any water apart from that clinging to it after washing. Squeeze excess water from cooked spinach by pressing between two plates or pushing into the base of a sieve.

CHICKEN SOUFFLÉ ROLL

1 pound spinach leaves

1 tablespoon butter or margarine

4 large eggs, separated

3 tablespoons grated Parmesan cheese

FILLING

¼ pound mushrooms, chopped

1 onion, chopped

1 tablespoon butter or margarine

3 tablespoons flour

½ cup milk

½ pound cooked diced chicken

2 tablespoons cream cheese

3 tablespoons sour cream

1 tablespoon Dijon mustard

freshly ground pepper

pinch nutmeg

CREAM OF SPINACH SOUP

2 pounds spinach or Swiss chard

2 tablespoons butter or margarine

1 small onion, finely chopped

3 tablespoons flour

1¼ cups chicken stock

1¼ cups milk

¼ teaspoon nutmeg

freshly ground pepper

1 Wash spinach well. Place in large pan with about 3 tablespoons water. Cook until tender — about 5 minutes. Drain well. Rub through a sieve or purée in a food processor. Set aside.

2 Sauté onion in butter until soft and transparent. Stir in flour. Remove pan from

heat and blend in stock and milk. Return to low heat, stirring continuously until mixture boils and thickens.

3 Stir in spinach purée, nutmeg and seasoning. Heat gently. Serve immediately.

SERVES 4

SCALLOP AND SPINACH QUICHE

PASTRY

2½ cups sifted flour

1½ sticks butter or margarine, cut in ½-inch bits

1 egg yolk

squeeze lemon juice

1 to 3 tablespoons ice water

FILLING

1 small onion, finely chopped

1 tablespoon butter or margarine

½ pound spinach leaves, shredded

3 eggs

1 cup cream

1 cup milk

freshly ground black pepper

pinch grated nutmeg

¼ pound scallops, cleaned

¼ cup Gruyère cheese, sliced

1 TO PREPARE PASTRY: Sift flour into a bowl. Add butter. Rub into flour, using fingertips, until mixture resembles bread crumbs.

2 Combine egg yolk, lemon juice and half the water. Sprinkle over flour. Stir to form a soft, pliable dough. Add extra water if necessary. Knead lightly. Wrap in plastic wrap. Rest in the refrigerator for 30 minutes.

3 Roll out pastry to line an 11-inch quiche pan.

4 TO PREPARE FILLING: Cook onion in butter until transparent. Add spinach. Cook for 3 minutes. Cool slightly.

5 Place spinach mixture in a bowl with eggs, cream, milk and seasoning. Beat well until combined.

6 Pour spinach mixture into pastry shell. Place scallops and cheese on top. Bake in a 375°F oven for 35 to 40 minutes or until set. Serve with a tossed salad.

SERVES 4 TO 6

Roll out pastry and line flan tin. Neaten edges with rolling pin.

Combine spinach mixture with egg and cream mixture.

Place scallops and cheese on top and bake in a moderately hot oven.

STEP-BY-STEP TECHNIQUES

CABBAGE ROLLS

1 large cabbage

FILLING
2 cups water
3 tablespoons uncooked long grain rice
1 pound lean ground beef
1 onion, finely chopped

SAUCE
2 carrots, scraped and grated
1 onion, chopped
4 tablespoons tomato purée
1 cup water or stock

1 Remove any damaged cabbage leaves. Fill a large saucepan with boiling water. Carefully separate cabbage leaves one by one and immerse in boiling water. When the inner leaves become difficult to separate, immerse the whole head in the boiling water for a minute or two, remove, and carefully take off more leaves until they become too small to use for stuffing. (The remainder of the cabbage head can be chopped and used in soup.) Soak the single leaves in the boiling water for about 10 minutes or until they are no longer crisp.

2 TO PREPARE FILLING: Place water in a saucepan and bring to the boil. Add rice. Boil, uncovered, for about 12 minutes. Drain and set aside.

3 Combine ground beef, onion and rice. Mix until well blended.

4 Drain cabbage leaves. Place one spoonful of stuffing in each leaf. Wrap into a tight package, tucking in the ends. Place rolls in a large casserole dish, stacking if necessary.

5 TO PREPARE SAUCE: Combine carrot, onion, tomato purée and water or stock, and pour over cabbage rolls.

Place spoonful of filling on blanched cabbage leaf.

Tuck in the ends.

Roll to form a tidy package.

6 Cook, covered, in a 350°F oven for about 45 minutes. If necessary, add a little more water and cook uncovered for 20 minutes more or until soft and meat is cooked. Serve cabbage rolls with sauce and vegetables.

SERVES 6

CHINESE GREEN SOUP

1 tablespoon oil

1 clove garlic, crushed

½ teaspoon grated ginger

6 cups hot chicken or vegetable stock

1 cup rice

1 small head Chinese cabbage, finely shredded

6 scallions, finely chopped

1 tablespoon dry sherry

½ teaspoon sesame oil

1 Heat oil in a heavy pot. Cook garlic and ginger 1 minute.

2 Pour in hot stock and rice. Simmer until rice is just tender.

3 Add cabbage and scallions. Simmer for 5 minutes. Stir in sherry and sesame oil. Serve hot.

SERVES 4 TO 6

TOFU SPINACH SOUFFLÉ

1 pound spinach

1½ tablespoons oil or ghee

1 teaspoon dried thyme

1 teaspoon dried oregano

1 to 2 cakes tofu

½ cup water

1 teaspoon kelp powder (see Note)

½ teaspoon freshly ground black pepper to taste

4 egg whites

1 Tear spinach leaves from stems and wash well. Chop very finely with a sharp knife or in a food processor.

2 Heat the oil in a pan. Cook the spinach for 5 minutes with the thyme and oregano. Drain off excess liquid by pressing between two plates.

3 Process tofu with water and dashi in a food processor or blender with pepper. Blend with the spinach. Allow to cool.

4 Beat egg whites until stiff and gently fold them through the spinach mixture. Lightly oil a soufflé dish. Fill with the spinach mixture.

5 Bake in a 375°F oven for 30 to 35 minutes or until the soufflé is well risen and firm to the touch. Serve immediately with salad or vegetables.

NOTE: Dashi (or kelp powder) is available from most Asian groceries and many supermarkets.

SERVES 4

SORREL SOUP

1½ tablespoons butter

1 large onion, thinly sliced

1 stick celery, chopped

2 pickled cucumbers, sliced

20 sorrel leaves, coarsely shredded

7 cups beef stock

1 egg

3 tablespoons sour cream

1 Melt butter in a large saucepan and sauté onion and celery for about 10 minutes or until softened. Onions should not brown.

2 Stir in cucumber and sorrel. Add stock and bring to the boil. Cover and simmer for 15 to 20 minutes.

3 Whisk egg lightly in a cup and add a little of the hot soup, slowly, while continuing to whisk. Add egg mixture to the soup stirring constantly. Do not allow soup to boil once the egg has been added.

4 Serve with sour cream if desired.

SERVES 4

CABBAGE ACCOMPANIMENT

Cabbage is delicious shredded and sautéed in butter with a little chopped onion, apple and a dash of vinegar.

WHAT'S IN A NAME?

Spinach and Swiss chard are often confused. Spinach has delicate dark green leaves and dark stems, and Swiss chard has larger, strongly veined, darker green leaves with white or red stems. It also has a much stronger flavor.

CHEESE AND SPINACH GNOCCHI

½ pound spinach leaves

1½ sticks butter or margarine, melted

1 pound ricotta cheese

½ cup grated Parmesan cheese

3 egg yolks, beaten

6 tablespoons plain flour

freshly ground black pepper

pinch nutmeg

½ cup fresh tomato sauce (see Note)

extra grated Parmesan for dusting

1 Wash spinach. Remove stems. Chop roughly. Cook for 3 minutes in half the melted butter. Shake pan to prevent sticking. All liquid should evaporate.

2 Cool and combine with ricotta and Parmesan cheese. Add beaten egg yolks, flour and seasonings. Process until smooth in a food processor. Chill for 30 minutes.

3 Prepare gnocchi by using 2 teaspoons to form mixture into small egg-shapes. Roll shapes lightly in flour. Cook gnocchi a few at a time in simmering salt water for 12 minutes. Gnocchi will float when cooked. Make sure they do not stick to each other.

4 Remove with a slotted spoon. Place them into a shallow casserole brushed with melted butter. Pour over tomato sauce. Dust with extra Parmesan cheese. Bake in a 375°F oven for 15 minutes or until cheese begins to brown.

NOTE: To prepare tomato sauce: Heat ½ cup olive oil in a frying pan. Sauté 1 chopped onion, 1 clove crushed garlic and ½ cup chopped parsley until onion is tender. Add 2 pounds peeled and chopped tomatoes with a pinch of sugar and seasonings to taste. Simmer for 45 minutes, stirring occasionally. Cool slightly. Purée in a food processor. The sauce may be stored, covered, in the refrigerator for a few days.

SERVES 6

LEAFY GREENS

Ensure all 'leafy greens' are well washed before using.

BASIL AND PASTA SALAD

2 cups fusilli or rotelle

¼ green cabbage, finely shredded

6 radishes, thinly sliced

1 small green pepper, thinly sliced

1 pint cherry tomatoes, halved if large

1 ripe avocado, sliced

½ seedless cucumber, thinly sliced

½ bunch chives and extra basil leaves to garnish

DRESSING

2 bunches fresh basil

4 cloves garlic, peeled

2 teaspoons Dijon mustard

juice ½ lemon

¾ cup olive oil

freshly ground black pepper

1 Cook pasta in boiling water until *al dente* (see Note). Drain well. Set aside to cool.

2 TO PREPARE DRESSING: Wash basil and strip leaves from stalks (reserve a few for garnish). Place leaves in the container of a food processor with garlic, mustard and half the lemon juice. Process until finely chopped.

3 Slowly add oil to the container with the motor still running. Process until dressing thickens. Add seasonings and remaining lemon juice to taste.

4 Toss all salad ingredients together in a bowl with dressing. Snip chives over salad. Garnish with reserved basil leaves.

NOTE: *al dente* means 'to the tooth'. Pasta should be tender with a slightly tender center.

SERVES 6

 COOKING IN STOCK

Try cooking cabbage and Brussels sprouts in stock for a change. Cabbage loses about half its bulk during cooking.

Basil and Pasta Salad

RED CABBAGE NUT SLAW WITH TAHINI ORANGE DRESSING

3 cups shredded red cabbage

1 cup shredded green cabbage

½ cup whole toasted blanched almonds

BASE DRESSING

3 tablespoons cream

1 tablespoon tarragon vinegar

1 teaspoon prepared mustard

¼ teaspoon garlic salt

TAHINI ORANGE DRESSING

3 tablespoons tahini

3 tablespoons water

juice and finely grated rind 1 orange

1 Combine red and green cabbage. Wash, drain and chill in refrigerator.

2 Combine base dressing ingredients in a screw-top jar. Shake well.

3 Toss cabbage with dressing and ¼ cup almonds. Pile into salad bowl. Top with remaining almonds.

4 Whisk together ingredients for Tahini Orange Dressing. Drizzle over salad to serve.

SERVES 6

Orange and Spinach Salad

ORANGE AND SPINACH SALAD

½ bunch spinach

4 scallions, chopped

¼ cup toasted flaked almonds (see Note)

2 oranges, peeled and segmented

3 tablespoons olive oil

1 tablespoon vinegar

1 tablespoon lemon juice

freshly ground black pepper, to taste

pinch dry mustard

1 Wash the spinach and remove stems. Shred and drain in a colander.

2 Mix together the spinach, scallions and almonds. Place on a serving dish. Arrange the sliced oranges over the spinach.

3 Whisk together the oil, vinegar, lemon juice, pepper and mustard and pour over the salad. Chill for 1 hour before serving.

NOTE: Toast almonds by placing in a dry frying pan and tossing over a medium heat until golden.

SERVES 4

GLAZED BRUSSELS SPROUTS

2 pints Brussels sprouts

1½ cups chicken stock

⅔ cup honey

pinch ground cloves

1½ tablespoons lemon juice

fresh sage, to garnish

1 Trim Brussels sprouts and cut a cross into the base. Blanch the sprouts briefly. Drain.

2 Place sprouts in a heavy saucepan. Cover with chicken stock and add honey and cloves. Cook until just tender.

COOKING CABBAGE

Remove the hard center core of the cabbage with a sharp knife. Slice the cabbage into two, then cut out the core working diagonally from the center of each cabbage. This will ensure that the leaves cook more evenly.

3 Remove sprouts. Keep warm while reducing liquid by boiling briskly. When liquid has halved in quantity, add lemon juice. Pour mixture over sprouts. Serve garnished with sage.

SERVES 6 TO 8

FENNEL SAUTÉ

3 heads fennel

4 tablespoons butter or margarine

freshly ground black pepper, to taste

grated rind and juice ½ lemon

1 tablespoon chopped fresh parsley

fresh chives, to garnish

1 Wash and string fennel. Cut into thin vertical slices. Melt the butter in a pan. Add the fennel, cover and cook for 5 minutes.
2 Remove the lid. Cook for a further 5 minutes. Transfer to a serving dish. Keep warm.
3 Add all the remaining ingredients to the pan. Heat through. Pour over the fennel. Serve garnished with chives.

SERVES 4

RED CABBAGE WITH SOUR CREAM

1½ tablespoons sunflower oil

1 red cabbage, shredded

1 onion, chopped

1 clove garlic, crushed

1 tablespoon tomato purée

1 tablespoon freshly squeezed lemon juice

3 tablespoons sour cream

1 Heat oil in a large skillet. Add cabbage, onion and garlic. Sauté until the cabbage has wilted.
2 Add tomato purée and lemon juice. Cover and simmer for approximately 10 minutes or until tender.

3 Remove from heat. Stir in sour cream immediately before serving. This dish goes well with meat rissoles.

SERVES 6 TO 8

BELGIAN ENDIVE WITH MUSTARD CREAM

2 tablespoons butter or margarine

1 onion, thinly sliced

4 endive, washed

1 cup chicken stock

¼ cup white wine

juice 1 lemon

½ cup cream

1 tablespoon Dijon mustard

freshly ground black pepper

1 slice boiled ham, cut into strips

3 tablespoons chopped fresh parsley

1 Sauté onion in butter until tender. Add endive and cook over low heat for 3 to 4 minutes.
2 Pour in stock, wine and lemon juice. Simmer over low heat for 15 to 20 minutes or until tender.
3 Remove endive from pan with a slotted spoon. Transfer to a greased shallow ovenproof dish. Cover and keep warm.
4 Rapidly boil remaining liquid until reduced to approximately ½ cup. Stir in cream, mustard and seasoning. Simmer for 4 to 5 minutes. Spoon cream sauce over endive. Top with ham and parsley. Serve as a meal accompaniment.

SERVES 4

 WHITE LEAF

Witloof (Belgian endive or chicory) means 'white leaf'. Its flavor combines well with a whole range of flavors. Witloof is excellent in salads or served steamed with a sauce. Avoid any with discolored, wilted or loosely packed leaves. Remove the center core of the witloof, which tends to be bitter, by using the point of a knife.

SALADE NIÇOISE

4 tomatoes, quartered

1 medium onion, sliced thinly

1 green pepper, sliced

1 red pepper, chopped

1 bunch curley endive or leaf lettuce,
washed and torn

1 romaine lettuce, washed and torn

½ pound new potatoes, cooked
and diced

1½ tablespoons finely chopped
basil

1 can tuna fish, drained and flaked

6 anchovy fillets, chopped

12 black olives, halved

¼ cup vinaigrette dressing

1 tablespoon capers

2 or 3 hard-boiled eggs, quartered

1 Place vegetables in a large salad bowl.
Toss to combine.

2 Fork through the tuna, anchovies and
olives. Pour over vinaigrette. Toss well.
Serve salad chilled, garnished with capers
and eggs.

SERVES 6

PAN BAGNIA

What could be more perfect for picnics?

1 long French bread

1 clove garlic, peeled

a little olive oil

3 hard-boiled eggs, peeled and sliced

2 ripe tomatoes, thinly sliced

½ bunch radishes, washed and sliced

One 3-ounce can anchovies, drained

black olives, halved and pitted

freshly ground black pepper

1 small butter lettuce, torn into
bite-sized pieces

1 Slice bread stick through horizontally
and remove some of the center to make
room for the filling. Rub the inside of the
bread with the cut clove of garlic, and
sprinkle with a little olive oil.

2 Arrange all the ingredients on the bottom
half of the bread stick. Season with pepper,
cover with the top half and tie in place.

3 Wrap in wax paper. Serve cut into slices.

SERVES 2

Salade Niçoise

EXOTIC FLOWER SALAD

1 large mango

1 tablespoon lemon juice

1 tablespoon vegetable oil

¼ pound button mushrooms, wiped and cut into quarters

freshly ground black pepper

2 heads leaf lettuce, leaves rinsed and chilled

1 Belgian endive, leaves separated

3 tablespoons pine nuts

1 tablespoon chopped fresh herbs

1 cup snow peas, trimmed

½ cup French dressing

1 Peel mango. Cut a thick slice from each side of the pit and set aside for the salad. Cut remaining flesh from the mango and purée. Add lemon juice and oil, and blend, adjusting the consistency to make a creamy mayonnaise.

2 Combine mayonnaise, mushrooms and pepper and toss lightly.

3 Arrange lettuce leaves and endive on individual plates in colorful flower shapes with the mushroom mixture in the center. Sprinkle with pine nuts and herbs.

4 Cut the thick mango slices into petal shapes, and arrange on the plates with the snow peas. Drizzle a little French dressing over each salad just before serving.

Exotic Flower Salad

CROPS FROM VINES

Zucchini are available in dark green, pale green, yellow, striped and mottled varieties all year. Look for firm, small to medium-sized zucchini with smooth skins.

Squash also come in a wonderful range of colors and can be bought in a 'button' or baby variety. Cook whole, halved, quartered or sliced in similar ways to zucchini.

Chayotes, known in the South as mirlitons, are mainly available during the winter months and can be used in soups, pickles, stir-fries and gratins.

Pumpkins and winter squashes come in a variety of shapes and colors. Some have edible skins. Others have sturdy skins which make spectacular containers for soup. Pumpkins can also be carved to make Jack O' Lantern candle holders for Halloween.
Squash is easy to grow and can be stored whole for up to two months, which makes them an ideal choice for the home gardener.

Bright green okra has a sticky texture and will keep for only a few days, even if refrigerated. The pods should be trimmed and used sliced or whole.

🌿 OKRA IDEAS

If cooking okra whole, slice off the tip and the stem end. Cut away as little as possible so that the internal sack, containing seeds and gummy liquid, is not pierced.

PASTRY SHELLS FOR VEGETABLES

¼ pound butter or margarine, cut in pieces
1 egg yolk
2½ cups sifted flour
¼ cup ice water

1 Blend butter and egg yolk together in a food processor. Add flour and water. Process until mixture just combines.
2 Remove. Knead into a ball but do not handle too much. Wrap in plastic wrap. Rest in refrigerator for 30 minutes.
3 Cut wax paper to fit individual tartlet tins. Grease lightly.
4 Roll out pastry on a floured surface. Cut into large circles. Ease pastry into tins. Trim edges with rolling pin. Chill for 10 minutes.
5 Place prepared wax paper (greased side to pastry) in tins. Weight with beans. Bake blind for 5 minutes in a 450°F oven.
6 Remove paper and beans. Lower temperature to 350°F. Cook for another 10 minutes or until golden. Cool slightly then unmold. Pastry shells can be stored in an airtight container until they are needed.

MAKES 8

RATATOUILLE TARTLETS

1 onion, sliced in rings

3 tablespoons olive oil

2 cloves garlic, crushed

2 zucchini, cut into slices

1 sweet pepper, seeded

One 14-ounce can tomatoes

1 small eggplant, diced

bouquet garni of 3 marjoram sprigs, 2 thyme sprigs, 1 parsley sprig, ½ bay leaf

freshly ground black pepper, to taste

6 Pastry Shells (see recipe above)

1 Sauté onion in oil until tender. Add garlic. Cook for 1 minute. Stir in zucchini, pepper, tomatoes, eggplant, bouquet garni and seasoning.

2 Cover. Simmer for 15 minutes. Remove bouquet garni. When cool, fill the pastry shells. Serve.

SERVES 6

CREAM OF CHAYOTE SOUP

6 chayotes

1 onion, chopped

1 stalk celery, stringed and chopped

½ cup rice

7 cups stock (chicken or vegetable)

1 clove garlic, crushed

freshly ground black pepper, to taste

½ cup sour cream (optional)

sweet pepper, cut in strips

1 Peel the chayotes, remove the seed and chop roughly. Place chayotes, onion, celery, rice, stock, garlic and ground pepper in a large saucepan. Simmer for 45 minutes.

2 Cool and purée the soup in a blender, or through a sieve. Return mixture to saucepan.

3 Stir in the sour cream over low heat. Do not allow it to boil. Serve hot with a dollop of sour cream if desired. Garnish with strips of pepper.

SERVES 4 TO 6

OKRA CASSEROLE

1 eggplant

salt

2 carrots, sliced

2 potatoes, peeled and sliced

¼ cup olive oil

2 onions, peeled and sliced

4 zucchini, sliced

4 tomatoes, sliced

½ pound fresh or frozen okra, trimmed

chopped parsley

2 teaspoons oregano

¼ teaspoon nutmeg

freshly ground black pepper, to taste

1 Slice eggplant, sprinkle with salt, and allow to stand for 30 minutes.

2 Place carrots and potatoes in boiling water. Simmer for 5 minutes. Refresh under cold water, and drain.

3 Rinse eggplant. Pat dry. Heat oil in a frying pan. Sauté onions until tender. Remove from pan. Fry eggplant until golden.

4 In a deep casserole layer all vegetables, sprinkling each layer with a little parsley, oregano, nutmeg and pepper. Cover casserole. Bake in a 375°F oven for 1 hour or until tender.

SERVES 6

FOR A CHANGE

Chayotes make great chutneys. If you don't have a recipe, substitute it for the major ingredient in your favorite chutney or pickle recipe.

OKRA TIPS

Okra should be tender but retain a crunch when cooked. Try them deep-fried, as a side dish or in curries and casseroles.

Step-by-Step Techniques

SPIRALI AND ZUCCHINI SALAD

½ pound zucchini

salt

1 cup mushrooms, sliced

¼ pound whole wheat spirali, cooked

¾ cup cream

¼ cup crunchy peanut butter

½ cup mayonnaise

3 tablespoons lemon juice

1½ tablespoons honey

1½ tablespoons white vinegar

½ cup roasted peanuts

1 Wash and slice zucchini. Place on paper towels and sprinkle with salt. Allow to stand 30 minutes. Rinse under cold water. Pat dry.

2 Combine zucchini, mushrooms and spirali in salad bowl. Chill while preparing dressing.

3 Place all remaining ingredients except peanuts in a food processor. Process until smooth but not too thick. Coat salad lightly with dressing.

4 Chill well. Serve garnished with peanuts. Extra dressing will keep well in the refrigerator.

SERVES 6

 ZUCCHINI VERSATILITY

Zucchini are wonderful as a main meal or appetizer stuffed with meat, bean, vegetable or cheese mixtures. Zucchini are best used with their skins on.

Sprinkle sliced zucchini with salt.

Combine zucchini, mushrooms and spirali.

Coat salad lightly with dressing.

BAKED ZUCCHINI IN SOUR CREAM

1 pound zucchini

6 tablespoons cream cheese

1 onion, finely chopped

freshly ground black pepper

½ cup sour cream

paprika

1 Place zucchini in boiling water. Reduce heat. Simmer 5 minutes. Drain well.

2 Cut in half lengthwise. Scoop seeds into a small bowl. Mix these with cream cheese, onion and seasoning.

3 Spoon mixture into zucchini. Arrange in buttered casserole dish. Spoon sour cream over zucchini.

4 Dust with paprika. Bake uncovered in a 350°F oven for 8 to 10 minutes to heat through.

SERVES 4 TO 6

BABY YELLOW AND GREEN SQUASH

2 pounds mixed green and yellow squash

4 tablespoons butter or margarine

1 tablespoon orange juice

orange peel cut into fine threads, blanched, for garnish

1 Wash and trim squash. Cook in boiling water for 5 to 6 minutes, or until crisp but tender. Refresh under cold water and drain.

2 Just before serving, melt butter. Add squash and orange juice. Heat through. Garnish with orange threads. Serve.

NOTE: If squash are medium-sized, cut into vertical slices.

SERVES 6 TO 8

COURGETTES AU BEURRE

1½ pounds zucchini

6 tablespoons butter or margarine

1 tablespoon chopped parsley

1 teaspoon chopped basil

freshly ground black pepper, to taste

1 Trim zucchini. Wash and dry. Cut into ¾-inch lengths. Drop into boiling water for five minutes. Drain well. Refresh under cold water.

2 Return to pan with butter, parsley, basil and pepper. Reheat. Serve hot sprinkled lightly with salt.

SERVES 6

CHILLED PUMPKIN SOUP

2 pounds pumpkin, peeled, seeded and diced

4½ cups chicken stock (see Note)

1 onion, chopped

4 scallions, sliced

freshly ground black pepper, to taste

¼ cup heavy cream

chives, to garnish

1 Cook pumpkin in water until tender. Drain, cool and purée in a blender or food processor.

2 Cook the stock with onion and scallions for 15 minutes. Cool and strain.

3 Blend the pumpkin into the stock. Season to taste. Cover and chill. Serve with a swirl of cream and chives to garnish.

NOTE: Fresh or canned stock may be used.

SERVES 6

 **EDIBLE FLOWERS**

The flowers of the zucchini make attractive edible garnishes for appetizers, main meals and salads.

FIRM BUT TENDER

Never cook pumpkin to a mush — it should retain its shape.

STUFFED CUCUMBER

1 seedless cucumber (see Note)

1 small bunch watercress

3 ounces fresh or canned crabmeat

¼ teaspoon grated fresh ginger

3 teaspoons soy sauce

1 Trim cucumber. Cut a lengthwise slit down cucumber only as deep as the seeds. Try to avoid halving cucumber. Using the handle of a teaspoon, scrape out and discard 'seeds'.

2 Pick over watercress and discard yellow leaves and stalks. Blanch sprigs in boiling water for 30 seconds only. Refresh immediately with cold water. Drain thoroughly.

3 Discard any cartilage from crabmeat. Drain well, squeezing out all liquid. Combine crab and ginger.

4 Holding cucumber slightly open, spoon crab mixture into cavity. Top with watercress leaves, reserving some for garnish. Press cucumber together gently. Wrap securely in plastic wrap. Refrigerate for 30 minutes.

5 Cut cucumber in ¾-inch slices. Arrange on a serving plate. Sprinkle with soy sauce. Garnish with remaining watercress sprigs.

NOTE: 'Seedless' cucumbers have seeds, but they are soft and edible.

SERVES 4 TO 6

COOKING TIP

If using these vegetables in casseroles or curries, they should be added towards the end of cooking time as they require very little cooking.

PUMPKIN TRIANGLES

1½ pounds pumpkin, peeled, seeded and chopped

1 large onion, chopped

1 clove garlic, crushed

¼ pound butter or margarine

1 cup Parmesan cheese

½ cup fresh bread crumbs

½ cup sour cream

2 egg yolks

freshly ground black pepper, to taste

¼ teaspoon cinnamon

½ cup oil

1 packet filo pastry

1 Cook pumpkin until tender. Mash well. Gently sauté the onion and garlic in 4 tablespoons butter until soft. Combine pumpkin with ⅓ cup Parmesan cheese, bread crumbs, sour cream, egg yolks and seasoning. Set aside to cool.

2 Melt remaining butter. Combine with oil. Liberally brush over 2 sheets of filo pastry. Place the pastry sheets one on top of the other. Cut into 3-inch wide strips. Keep the other sheets of filo pastry covered with a damp cloth to prevent drying out.

3 Place 2 teaspoons of filling in the bottom left corner of each strip. Fold over to form a triangle. Continue folding the triangle to the end of the strip. Place, seam down, on greased baking tray. Brush with butter mixture. Follow this procedure for the remaining filling and pastry.

4 Sprinkle the triangles with Parmesan cheese. Bake in a 375°F oven for about 15 minutes or until golden. These make great appetizers.

MAKES ABOUT 30 TRIANGLES

STUFFED SUMMER SQUASH

4 tablespoons butter or margarine

⅔ pound ground meat (beef, pork or lamb)

1 onion, chopped

3 tablespoons cooked long grain rice

3 tablespoons finely chopped mushrooms

1 large summer squash

1 TO PREPARE STUFFING: Heat butter in a pan. Stir-fry meat, onion, rice and mushrooms until meat is well browned.

2 Cut end off squash. Scoop out the seeds. Spoon in prepared stuffing. Place squash in a greased casserole dish. Cover and bake in a 350°F oven for 40 to 50 minutes.

3 Slice in pieces about ¾-inch across to serve.

SERVES 4

Stuffed Summer Squash

🌱 **DEGORGE**

If zucchini are old, it is a good idea to slice and sprinkle with salt and allow to stand for about 20 to 30 minutes before using (known as 'degorge'). This will draw out excess water.

Cook cucumber in stock until tender.

Stir in yogurt mixture and chopped coriander.

Add ice water and mix well.

YOGURT AND CUCUMBER SOUP

1 cucumber, peeled, seeded and diced

2 cups chicken or vegetable stock

2 cloves garlic, crushed

2½ cups plain yogurt

juice ½ lemon

½ to 1 tablespoon finely chopped coriander

1 cup ice water

4 to 6 very thin slices lemon

3 tablespoons chopped walnuts

1 Cook cucumber in stock until just tender. Refrigerate till cold.

2 Mix garlic with yogurt and lemon juice. Stir in coriander, cucumber and stock. Pour in ice water. Mix well. Serve topped with lemon slices and chopped walnuts.

SERVES 4 TO 6

TANGY MANGO AND CUCUMBER SOUP

3 scallions, trimmed

1 mango, peeled, pitted and puréed

½ cup lemon juice

½ cup orange and mango juice

½ cup plain low-fat yogurt

1 clove garlic, crushed

1½ cucumbers, peeled, seeded and grated

freshly ground pepper

½ red pepper, finely diced

1 In a food processor or blender, process scallions, mango, lemon juice, orange and mango juice, yogurt and garlic.

2 Transfer to a serving bowl. Add grated cucumber and seasoning.

3 Chill until ready to serve. Garnish with sliced cucumber and red pepper.

SERVES 4

PUMPKIN TIMBALES

2 cups of puréed steamed pumpkin, dry, not moist

4 eggs, beaten

1½ cups cream

2 tablespoons butter or margarine, melted

½ teaspoon nutmeg

½ teaspoon cinnamon

freshly ground black pepper, to taste

Italian parsley for garnish

1 Butter 6 individual soufflé dishes or molds. Combine pumpkin with eggs, cream, butter, nutmeg, cinnamon and pepper. Blend well.

2 Pour mixture into greased molds. Place molds in a baking dish. Pour in enough boiling water to reach halfway up the sides of the molds.

3 Cover each mold with buttered wax paper. Cook in a 400°F oven for 25 to 30 minutes or until set.

4 Allow to rest 5 minutes before unmolding. Garnish each with Italian parsley.

NOTE: To unmould: Run the point of a knife around the edge of each mold. Invert onto serving plate. Shake gently. Carefully remove mold.

SERVES 6

Tangy Mango and Cucumber Soup

 EASY PEEL

Peel pumpkin by cutting into easily held sections. Cut off the skin in strips with a sharp knife. Scrape away the seeds and fibers with a knife or a spoon.

Sweet Vegetables

Carrots, zucchini and pumpkin are perhaps the most popular vegetables used in sweet dishes. They are commonly seen in cakes, but pumpkin is also often seen in pies, mousse and scones.

Cakes, slices and breads are the perfect places to use these sweet vegetables, which have the ability to blend with the other ingredients involved and add flavor, moistness and a natural sweetness to these recipes. Following is a selection of sweet sensations we know you'll love.

ZUCCHINI CAKE

6 tablespoons butter or margarine

¾ cup sugar

grated rind 1 orange

2 eggs

1¾ cups self-rising flour, sifted

1 cup grated zucchini

½ cup chopped pecans

3 tablespoons orange juice

3 tablespoons milk

½ teaspoon cinnamon

1 Cream butter and sugar together until light and fluffy. Beat in rind. Add eggs one at a time, beating well after each addition. Lightly blend in all remaining ingredients.
2 Pour into a greased loaf pan. Bake in a 350°F oven for 45 minutes or until a skewer inserted in the center of the cake comes out clean and dry.
3 Turn onto a wire rack to cool. Dust with confectioner's sugar. Served sliced with butter.

MAKES 1 CAKE

SUCCULENT CARROT SLICE

1¼ cups sifted flour

1¼ teaspoon baking powder

1 teaspoon bicarbonate of soda

¾ cup brown sugar

1 cup grated carrot

½ cup drained crushed pineapple

¼ cup chopped walnuts

2 eggs

7 tablespoons oil

¾ teaspoon each cinnamon and nutmeg

ICING

4 tablespoons butter or margarine

4 tablespoons cream cheese

2 cups confectioner's sugar, sifted

2 teaspoons orange or lemon juice

few drops vanilla extract

1 Sift flour, baking powder and bicarbonate of soda together into a bowl. Blend in all remaining ingredients. Mix well.
2 Pour into a greased and lined 9-inch square pan. Bake in a 350°F oven for 30 to 35 minutes or until a skewer inserted into the center of the cake comes out clean and dry. Turn onto a wire rack to cool.
3 TO PREPARE ICING: Cream butter and cream cheese together until smooth. Gradually blend in confectioner's sugar, juice and vanilla until creamy. Spread over cooled cake.

MAKES 1 CAKE

PUMPKIN PIE

PASTRY

1 cup self-rising flour

1 cup whole wheat flour

¼ pound butter or margarine

1 egg yolk

3 tablespoons lemon juice

cold water

FILLING

1½ cups cooked pumpkin

¼ cup cream

2 eggs, separated

1½ tablespoons brown sugar

¼ teaspoon each nutmeg and ground ginger

1 TO PREPARE PASTRY: Sift flours into a bowl, returning any husks. Add butter. Rub in using fingertips until mixture resembles bread crumbs.

2 Mix yolk, juice and enough cold water into flour to form a firm but pliable dough. Wrap in plastic wrap. Rest in the refrigerator for about 20 minutes.

3 Roll out on a lightly floured surface to fit an 8-inch pie tin. Ease pastry into plate. Trim and decorate edges. Refrigerate for 15 minutes.

4 TO PREPARE FILLING: Place pumpkin in a food processor with cream, egg yolks, sugar and spices. Process until smooth. Transfer to a bowl.

5 Beat egg whites until stiff peaks form. Fold lightly into pumpkin mixture. Pour into pastry shell.

6 Bake in a 350°F oven for 35 minutes or until pastry is golden and filling is set. Serve warm with whipped cream.

SERVES 4 TO 6

 NOTE

Commercially prepared piecrust may be used. Cook pumpkin by boiling, steaming or in the microwave. Drain well.

Succulent Carrot Slice

ONIONS & OTHER ALLIUMS

Onions, scallions and leeks, as well as garlic, have played an indispensable part in cooking for centuries, both as a flavoring and as a main ingredient.

There are many varieties of onions, but those most widely available are white onions, the strong yellow onions, the small 'pickling' onion and the milder and sweeter Italian onion with its purply-red colored skin. Available all year, onions should be well-shaped and firm. The outer skin should be dry and papery. Avoid any that are soft or blemished. They will keep for up to 2 months if stored in a cool, dark place.

Scallions, as they are commonly known, are also available all year and are delicious in salads, stir-fries, in sauces, with fish, in breads and so on. They should have bright green tops that are not wilted and the root end should be white.

Leeks are delicately onion-flavored and lend themselves beautifully to cookery, whether it be in casseroles, quiches, soups, sauces or gratins. They are available all year and should be crisp with a white root end and bright green tops.

15 minutes. Cool slightly. Purée in a food processor, then strain through a sieve.

3 Add milk and cream. Reheat gently. Cool and chill thoroughly.

4 Serve Vichyssoise in chilled bowls. Float a little whipped cream and curly leek needles on top of soup.

NOTE: Prepare leek needles from the soft green tops of the leek. Shred these finely and drop them into ice water so they will curl. Drain and use as a garnish.

SERVES 6

PARSLEY AND WALNUT SOUP

½ pound shelled walnuts
4 tablespoons butter or margarine
2 leeks, sliced and washed
1½ bunches Italian parsley leaves
2 cups chicken stock
freshly ground black pepper, to taste
4 tablespoons cream

1 Blanch walnuts in boiling salted water for 3 minutes. Refresh under cold water. Rub the nuts in a dish towel, then between your fingers to remove skins.

2 Melt butter in heavy saucepan. Add leeks and parsley. Cover closely with a piece of wax paper. Cover with a lid. Sweat over a low heat for 5 minutes.

3 Remove paper. Add walnuts and chicken stock. Bring to the boil. Simmer for 10 minutes.

4 Blend soup until smooth in a food processor with seasoning. Return to saucepan. Reheat gently. Stir through cream.

SERVES 4

Vichyssoise

CLEAN LEEKS

Ensure leeks are thoroughly washed to remove accumulated dirt and grit. If leeks are to remain whole, do this by piercing the leek where the white joins the green with a sharp, pointed knife. Draw the knife to the top end to split the leaves open. Make a second slit at right angles to the first. Rinse the leek thoroughly in cold water.

VICHYSSOISE

1 white onion
4 leeks, well washed
4 tablespoons butter or margarine
4½ cups chicken stock
1 stalk celery, chopped
3 potatoes, peeled and thinly sliced
1 tablespoon chopped parsley
freshly ground black pepper, to taste
1¼ cups milk
1¼ cups cream

GARNISH
1 cup whipped cream
leek needles (see Note)

1 Slice the onion and white part of the leek finely. Melt butter in saucepan. Sauté onion and leek gently until tender. Do not let them brown.

2 Add chicken stock, celery, potatoes, chopped parsley and seasoning. Simmer for

THAI CHICKEN SALAD

4 to 6 boneless chicken breasts

¼ cup rice wine vinegar

3 tablespoons fresh coriander leaves

1½ tablespoons light soy sauce

1½ tablespoons raw sugar

1½ tablespoons sesame seed oil

DRESSING

3 tablespoons rice wine vinegar

1 tablespoon wasabi or chopped horseradish

1 teaspoon sugar

freshly ground black pepper, to taste

3 tablespoons walnut oil

SALAD VEGETABLES

1 small head romaine lettuce

2 tomatoes, peeled, seeded and cut into eighths

1 red and 1 green pepper, finely sliced

1 large carrot, julienned

½ bunch scallions, finely sliced on the diagonal

½ seedless cucumber, peeled and julienned

GARNISH

4 tablespoons each coriander, mint and basil

½ bunch chives

3 tablespoons sesame seeds, toasted

1 Cut each chicken breast into three long strips. Place in a glass or ceramic bowl with vinegar, coriander, soy sauce and sugar. Toss to combine. Cover and refrigerate overnight.

2 Heat sesame oil in a wok. Stir-fry chicken pieces over high heat until just cooked. Turn out onto a plate. Set aside.

3 TO PREPARE DRESSING: Combine first four ingredients in a bowl. Whisk in oil until combined.

4 Toss salad vegetables together with half the dressing. Arrange in the center of each individual plate with a few small romaine leaves. Divide chicken strips among the plates, arranging them over the salad. Sprinkle each plate with a little more dressing. Garnish each with fresh herbs and toasted sesame seeds.

SERVES 4 TO 6

ONION RAGOUT

6 tablespoons butter or margarine

2 pounds small onions, peeled

One 14½-ounce can tomatoes, drained

1¼ cups chicken stock

¼ cup white wine

2 cloves

1 bay leaf

small stick cinnamon

1 Melt butter in a heavy based saucepan. Fry whole onions until golden brown.

2 Add all remaining ingredients. Simmer for 45 minutes or until onions are tender.

SERVES 6 TO 8

PEELING ONIONS

When preparing onions, peel leaving the root intact. This will ensure that the onion does not fall apart during cooking.

Thai Chicken Salad

Scallop Bundles with Herb Cream Sauce

SCALLOP BUNDLES WITH HERB CREAM SAUCE

1 pound scallops

1 leek, rinsed and sliced

few peppercorns

bouquet garni

1 cup water

½ cup dry white wine

½ bunch chives, snipped

grated rind ½ lemon

1 teaspoon black sesame seeds

8 sheets filo pastry

4 tablespoons butter or margarine, melted

HERB CREAM SAUCE
reserved poaching liquid
1 cup crème fraîche
freshly ground black pepper
3 fresh sorrel leaves

1 Trim scallops. Place leek in a large saucepan with peppercorns, bouquet garni, water and white wine. Bring to the boil. Add scallops. Lower heat. Poach gently for 2 minutes. Leave to cool in the liquid. Drain well, reserving all poaching liquid with bouquet garni. Toss the scallops with chives, lemon rind and sesame seeds.

2 Take a sheet of filo pastry and brush liberally with melted butter. Cut into quarters. Lay the four squares one on top of the other. Cover remaining pastry with plastic wrap or a damp cloth while you prepare each bundle.

3 Spoon a tablespoon of the scallop filling onto the center of the pastry. Fold into a parcel. Secure the top with a soft piece of string.

4 Repeat with remaining pastry and scallop mixture. Place on a greased baking tray. Bake in a 375°F oven for 12 to 15 minutes or until golden and crisp. Remove string. Tie with a chive.

5 TO PREPARE HERB CREAM SAUCE: Reduce reserved poaching liquid to ⅔ cup by boiling rapidly. Remove bouquet garni. Strain into a measuring cup. Put crème fraîche and poaching liquid into a small saucepan. Bring to the boil with seasonings. Cut the sorrel leaves into strips. Add to the sauce just before serving.

6 Serve each individual plate with two scallop bundles sitting in a pool of hot sauce.

SERVES 2 AS AN APPETIZER

 CRÈME FRAÎCHE

Crème fraîche, available in many supermarkets, can be used to make a savory sauce, or sweetened with sugar. It will keep for 2 weeks in the refrigerator. To make 2 cups crème fraîche, beat 1¼ cups fresh cream with ¾ cup yogurt in a small bowl. Cover and refrigerate overnight.

RICE AND LEEKS

2 leeks, trimmed and washed

3 tablespoons olive oil

1 cup long grain rice

3 tomatoes, peeled and coarsely chopped

1 teaspoon brown sugar

freshly ground black pepper, to taste

1¾ cups boiling water

squeeze of lemon juice

1 Slice leeks into ½-inch pieces. Heat oil in large skillet. Add leeks, and fork through to break up slices. Cook, stirring occasionally, for 5 minutes.

2 Add rice. Mix through. Cook, stirring occasionally, until rice is opaque. Add tomatoes, sugar and seasoning. Pour in water.

3 Cook gently, covered, until all liquid is absorbed and rice is tender. Add more water if necessary. Sprinkle with lemon juice to serve.

SERVES 4

PISSALADIERE

QUICK DOUGH

2 cups self-rising whole wheat flour

4 tablespoons butter or margarine, cubed

⅓ cup milk

TOPPING

¼ cup oil

3 onions, peeled and sliced

½ pound tomatoes, peeled and sliced

freshly ground black pepper, to taste

½ pound mozzarella cheese, sliced

GARNISH

2 ounces anchovy fillets, drained

20 stuffed green olives

1 TO PREPARE QUICK DOUGH: Sift flour into a bowl. Add butter. Rub butter into flour using fingertips. Mix in milk to make a firm dough.

2 Turn dough onto lightly floured board. Knead until there are no cracks. Pat out to round shape 9 inches in diameter. Place on greased baking sheet.

3 Using forefinger and thumb, raise edge slightly by pinching the dough.

4 TO PREPARE TOPPING: Fry onions in oil until soft, but not browned. Spread onions over top of dough with tomato slices. Sprinkle with pepper. Top with cheese.

5 Bake in a 450°F oven for 20 minutes or until base is browned and cheese bubbling. For extra flavor, add garnish of anchovy fillets and olives. Cook further 10 minutes.

SERVES 2 TO 3

BELGIAN LEEK SOUP

4 tablespoons butter or margarine

2 or 3 large leeks, washed and sliced

1 pound potatoes, diced

7 cups beef stock

freshly ground black pepper, to taste

½ cup cream

6 slices toasted French bread

nutmeg

thin slices of leek for garnish

1 Melt butter in a large saucepan. Fry leeks gently for 3 minutes. Add potatoes, beef stock and seasoning. Bring to the boil.

2 Cover, reduce heat. Simmer for 40 minutes, stirring occasionally. Before serving, stir in cream.

3 Place one piece of toast in each soup bowl. Pour over the hot soup. Sprinkle lightly with nutmeg and thin slices of leek.

SERVES 6

PICKLED ONIONS

2 pounds small white onions

1 pound coarse salt

2½ quarts water

3 cups white vinegar

1 cup tarragon vinegar

3 tablespoons brown sugar

1 tablespoon black peppercorns

½ teaspoon ground allspice

2 whole cloves

1 cinnamon stick

1 Wash unpeeled onions and place in a bowl. Mix half the salt with half the water. Pour brine over onions to completely cover them. Weight with a plate to ensure onions are totally immersed. Leave for 12 hours.

2 Drain and peel onions. Place in a clean bowl. Mix remaining salt and water together. Pour over onions. Cover and leave for 24 hours.

3 Drain and wash onions. Pack into sterilized jars, leaving plenty of space at top.

4 Place vinegar, sugar, peppercorns, allspice, cloves and cinnamon stick in a saucepan. Stir over low heat till sugar dissolves. Bring to the boil. Reduce heat and simmer for 5 minutes.

5 Strain mixture through a fine sieve. Pour over onions until it comes at least ½ inch above them. Seal, label and leave for 3 months. Serve with salads, antipasto or on sandwiches.

MAKES 2 POUNDS

PROVENÇALE CHICKEN

8 chicken pieces

salt, pepper, cinnamon

¼ cup oil

12 small white onions, peeled

½ pound button mushrooms

1 green pepper, sliced

1 clove garlic, crushed

4 large tomatoes, peeled, seeded and chopped

½ cup white wine

1 cup tomato purée

1 bouquet garni

3 tablespoons parsley, chopped

16 black olives

1 Season chicken pieces with salt, pepper and cinnamon. Heat oil in skillet. Brown chicken pieces on all sides. Remove from pan. Drain on absorbent paper.

2 Lightly sauté onions, mushrooms, pepper and garlic. Remove and drain.

3 Sauté tomato. Stir in wine. Return vegetables to pan. Add tomato purée and bouquet garni. Heat gently.

4 Add chicken pieces to pan with sauce, and cook an additional 20 to 25 minutes until chicken is done. Remove bouquet garni. Arrange chicken on serving dish. Pour over sauce with vegetables. Sprinkle with parsley and olives. Serve hot with buttered pasta.

SERVES 4

GARLIC CLOVES

Peel garlic cloves by placing under the blade of a heavy knife. Press down firmly to split the skin. It is then easily peeled away.

USING LEEKS

Store them unwashed in a plastic bag in the refrigerator. When ready to use, remove leaves and thoroughly wash the bulbs to remove accumulated grit and dirt.

STEP-BY-STEP TECHNIQUES

NORWEGIAN FISH SOUP

2 tablespoons butter or margarine

2 leeks or 8 scallions, cleaned and finely
sliced

¾ pound potatoes, peeled and diced

1 stalk celery, diced

5½ cups water

freshly ground black pepper

1 pound white fish fillets (see Note)

1 tablespoon chopped dill, to garnish

1 Melt the butter in a large pan. Add leeks,
potatoes and celery. Cook over a low heat for
5 minutes. Blend in water and seasoning.
Bring to the boil. Reduce heat and simmer
for 10 minutes or until potatoes are almost
tender.

2 Check the fish for bones and cut into
1-inch pieces. Stir into the soup. Continue
simmering gently for about 5 minutes or
until the fish is tender. Serve hot sprinkled
with dill.

NOTE: Grouper, redfish, or cod would be
ideal.

SERVES 4

Norwegian Fish Soup

Add leeks, potatoes and celery to pan.

Add water and simmer.

Add fish to soup.

Crab in Pastry

COCK-A-LEEKIE

4 to 5 pound chicken

4½ cups chicken stock

½ cup pearl barley

bouquet garni

10 leeks, trimmed and washed

10 prunes, pitted and soaked

3 tablespoons chopped parsley

freshly ground black pepper, to taste

½ cup cream, optional

1 Simmer chicken in a large, partially covered saucepan with stock, barley and bouquet garni for 40 minutes.

2 Slice and rinse leeks thoroughly. Add them, with the prunes, to the stock. Cook for a further 15 minutes.

3 Discard the bouquet garni. Lift chicken from pot. Skin and bone chicken. Cut the meat into bite-sized pieces, returning these to the pan.

4 Chill soup then skim fat from the surface. Reheat, adding parsley and seasoning. Stir in cream. Bring to the boil. Serve with crusty bread.

SERVES 6

PEELING ONIONS

If onions are placed in the freezer for 15 minutes before peeling, tears during peeling should be reduced.

BOUQUET GARNI

A 'bouquet garni' is a seasoning made of celery, thyme, parsley and a bay leaf tied together with string, or a muslin bag containing parsley, thyme, bay and chervil. Always remove before serving. A commercial variety is also available in the herb and spice section of your supermarket.

CRAB IN PASTRY

1 package frozen puff pastry sheets, thawed

1 egg yolk, beaten

2 tablespoons butter or margarine

3 tablespoons oil

4 scallions, finely chopped

½ pound crabmeat, fresh or canned

¼ cup brandy

juice ½ lemon

pinch paprika

¼ cup cream

4 cooked shrimp, to garnish

1 On a lightly floured work surface, smooth out the pastry, and, with a sharp knife, cut out four 4-inch squares.

2 Make a shallow incision ½ inch from the borders to mark squares, which will be lifted off to form lids when cooked.

3 Place pastry on a dampened baking sheet. Refrigerate for 20 minutes. Brush top only with egg yolk. Bake in a 400°F oven for 5 minutes, then reduce the heat to 375°F for a further 20 minutes.

4 Take tray from oven and remove lids. Scrape out any uncooked pastry and return tray to oven for a further 5 minutes.

5 While pastry cases are baking for the final 5 minutes, prepare filling. Heat butter and oil in a pan. Sauté scallions until soft. Add crab, brandy, lemon juice, paprika and lastly cream. Heat through, stirring, over a gentle heat. Do not boil.

6 Divide filling among pastry cases. Place lids on top. Serve hot, garnished with shrimp. Serve with sautéed snow peas.

SERVES 4

LEEK ROULADE

3 leeks, sliced

4 eggs, separated

3 tablespoons Parmesan cheese, grated

3 tablespoons chives, chopped

3 slices bacon, chopped

1 tablespoon butter or margarine

½ cup mushrooms, chopped

1 teaspoon dry mustard

1 Line a jelly roll pan with oiled wax paper. Pre-heat oven to 400°F.

2 Boil leeks in water for 3 minutes. Drain well. Mix eggs yolks with half the cheese. Stir in leeks and chives.

3 Beat egg whites until stiff, and fold into leek mixture.

4 Spread mixture evenly over wax paper. Bake for 15 minutes until firm.

5 While roulade is cooking, sauté bacon in butter until browned. Add mushrooms. Cook 2 minutes. Stir in mustard.

6 When cooked, turn roulade out onto a clean, soft dish towel. Remove wax paper. Spread bacon mixture over the top. Sprinkle with remaining cheese. Beginning on the long side, using the towel, roll up as for a jelly roll. Serve sliced with salad.

SERVES 6

 NO MORE ONION ODOR

If you wash your hand in milk after peeling onions, the smell will be removed.

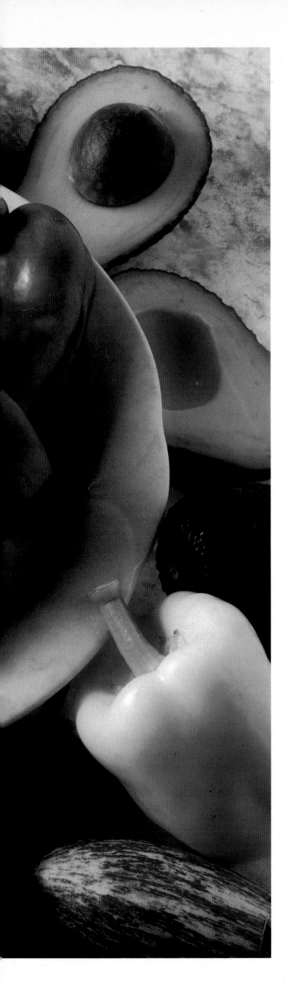

FRUITS OF THE EARTH

Eggplant comes in many shapes and sizes and is indeed a versatile vegetable. Look for shiny, unblemished, firm, dark purple specimens with fresh looking stalks. Delicious marinated, in an antipasto, as a dip, stuffed or deep-fried.

Raw or cooked, tomatoes have myriad uses in cookery. Today you can buy tomatoes in a wide range of sizes and shapes. If they are a little green, leave to ripen at room temperature on a window sill.

Colorful peppers come in red, green, yellow, orange, even purple and brown. Plentiful year round, they are perfect for summery salads or winter warmers. Look for firm, smooth, glossy specimens which have no blemishes.

Avocados, once a treat, are now plentiful. Also plentiful are recipes for using them. Although available year round, they are at their best in the cooler months. Delicious simply with a vinaigrette dressing, avocados make a creamy addition to many dishes.

EGGPLANT PURÉE

2 eggplants

juice 1 lemon

2 tablespoons oil

2 cloves garlic, crushed

3 tablespoons yogurt

¼ pound cream cheese

black olives for decoration

paprika, to garnish

1 Place eggplants on a baking sheet. Bake 1 hour in a 350°F oven. Cut in half. Scoop out the pulp and purée in a food processor or blender.

2 Add lemon juice, oil, garlic, yogurt and cream cheese. Process until smooth.

3 Place in a bowl. Chill for several hours. Garnish with olives and paprika. Eggplant purée can be served in the scooped out eggplant cases.

Eggplant Purée

RATATOUILLE

3 tomatoes, roughly chopped

½ small eggplant, sliced and cut in four

1 zucchini, sliced

1 carrot, peeled and sliced

¼ red pepper, sliced

¼ green pepper, sliced

1 onion, sliced

1 clove garlic, finely chopped

1 tablespoon chopped fresh basil

Place all the ingredients in a nonstick frying pan. Cook gently for 30 minutes.
Stir from time to time to prevent sticking. Serve as a side dish.

SERVES 2

MOUSSAKA

5 large eggplants, sliced and sprinkled with salt

3 tablespoons oil

4 tablespoons butter or margarine

3 pounds pound ground lamb or beef

4 onions, peeled and chopped

freshly ground black pepper to taste

½ teaspoon cinnamon

8 ripe tomatoes, peeled, seeded and chopped

½ cup chopped parsley

⅓ cup to ½ cup water

1 cup bread crumbs

1 cup grated Parmesan cheese

4 tablespoons grated tasty cheese

SAUCE

6 tablespoons butter or margarine

5 tablespoons plain flour

4½ cups milk

6 egg yolks, beaten

seasonings to taste

1 Rinse and dry eggplant slices after 15 minutes.

2 Heat oil in a frying pan. Cook eggplant until lightly browned on both sides. Remove. Drain on absorbent paper.

3 Melt butter in same pan. Brown meat. Add onions. Cook until onions golden. Stir in seasonings. Add tomatoes, parsley and water. Bring to boil. Simmer for 20 to 30 minutes.

4 Sprinkle half the bread crumbs into a large buttered baking dish. Layer meat, eggplant and half the cheeses.

5 **TO PREPARE SAUCE:** Melt butter in a saucepan. Add flour. Cook until mixture bubbles, then off-heat whisk in milk. Return to heat. Bring to boil, stirring continuously. Simmer 3 to 5 minutes.

6 Beat 3 tablespoons of the hot sauce into the eggs. Pour egg mixture back into remaining sauce, beating all the time. Season to taste. Pour sauce over moussaka. Sprinkle with remaining cheese and bread crumbs.

7 Bake in a 350°F oven for 1 hour, or until crust is crisp and brown. Cut into squares. Serve hot with salad or vegetables.

SERVES 4

PIZZAIOLA MUSSELS

18 large mussels

2 tablespoons butter or margarine

1 onion, chopped

1 clove garlic, crushed

2 tomatoes, peeled, seeded and chopped

1 bouquet garni

1 tablespoon lemon juice

freshly ground black pepper

1 tablespoon finely chopped parsley

½ cup grated cheese

Pizzaiola Mussels

1 Scrub mussels thoroughly. Remove beards. Discard any mussels with broken or open shells. Soak remainder in cold water for 20 minutes.

2 Heat butter in pan. Gently cook onion and garlic until tender. Add tomatoes, bouquet garni, lemon juice and seasoning. Cook for 5 minutes. Remove bouquet garni.

3 Open mussels with a sharp knife, starting at hinge and working round to join. Place open mussels on a flat ovenproof dish. Cover with tomato mixture.

4 Sprinkle with parsley and cheese. Bake in a 350°F oven for 8 minutes.

5 Serve immediately with crusty bread to soak up the sauce.

SERVES 2

HOT HANDS

Never put your hands near your eyes or mouth when handling fresh chiles. Wear rubber gloves to prevent burning or use the chopped fresh chile available in jars from your supermarket.

PILAF WITH EGGPLANT

4 small eggplants

3 tablespoons olive oil

2 tomatoes, peeled, seeded and chopped

1 clove garlic, crushed

1 cup long grain rice

freshly ground black pepper

2 cups hot chicken stock

1 Cut the eggplants in half lengthwise then into ½-inch thick slices. Sprinkle with salt. Set aside for 15 minutes. Rinse well. Pat dry with paper towels.

2 Heat the olive oil in a large casserole. Sauté the eggplant slices until lightly browned on both sides. Add tomatoes and garlic. Simmer over low heat for 5 minutes, stirring occasionally.

3 Add rice and seasoning. Combine thoroughly. Pour in the hot stock. Bring to the boil. Lower the heat. Simmer, covered, until the rice has absorbed all the liquid (about 25 minutes).

4 Place the casserole over the lowest possible heat. Cook 15 minutes more.

5 Serve hot or cold with a side dish of natural yogurt.

SERVES 4

TOMATO PERSILLES

2 ripe tomatoes

1 tablespoon pine nuts

½ tablespoon oil

½ tablespoon butter or margarine

¼ cup chopped parsley

1 clove garlic, crushed

freshly ground black pepper

1 Halve and seed tomatoes. Drain upside down on absorbent paper.

2 Cook pine nuts in oil until slightly colored. Drain.

3 Melt butter. Gently cook parsley and garlic. Season with pepper.

4 Brush outside skin of tomatoes with a little more oil. Place in ovenproof dish. Spoon parsley mixture into tomatoes. Top with pine nuts. Bake in a 350°F oven for 7 to 10 minutes or until just tender.

SERVES 2

FRESH TOMATO SOUP

2 tablespoons butter or margarine

1 onion, thinly sliced

1 carrot, peeled and thinly sliced

1 tablespoon flour

2 pounds tomatoes, peeled and quartered

3 cups chicken or vegetable stock

1 bay leaf

pinch ground mace

freshly ground black pepper

1 Melt butter in a heavy, medium pot. Add onion and carrot. Cover and cook over low heat for 5 to 10 minutes.

2 Remove pan from heat. Stir in flour. Add tomatoes, stock, bay leaf, mace and seasoning. Bring to boil, stirring. Simmer, covered, for 20 to 30 minutes.

3 Remove bay leaf. Purée the soup either in a food processor or blender, or by pressing through a sieve. Rinse out pot and return pureéd soup. Reheat before serving with crusty bread.

SERVES 6

STEP-BY-STEP TECHNIQUES

TUNA SALAD WITH GARLIC TOAST

1 eggplant

salt

3 tablespoons oil

One 6-ounce can tuna in oil, drained and flaked

2 stalks celery, chopped

4 tablespoons olive oil

1 tablespoon vinegar

½ teaspoon Dijon mustard

8 black olives

1 long French bread

1½ sticks butter or margarine

1 to 2 cloves garlic, crushed

Tuna Salad with Garlic Toast

1 Peel eggplant. Cut into cubes and sprinkle with salt. Leave for 30 minutes to draw out some of the liquid. Rinse well and pat dry.

2 Cook eggplant cubes quickly in hot oil. Drain well. When cool, toss with tuna and celery.

3 Whisk together olive oil, vinegar and mustard. Pour dressing over eggplant-tuna mix. Toss lightly. Garnish with olives. Refrigerate until required.

4 Slice bread. Combine butter and garlic. Coat each side of bread. Place on a baking sheet. Bake in a 375°F oven for 10 minutes or until brown and crisp. Serve immediately with tuna salad.

SERVES 4

Pat washed eggplant cubes dry.

Whisk together olive oil, vinegar and mustard to make dressing.

Place celery, tuna and eggplant cubes in a bowl.

DILL TOMATOES

4 large ripe tomatoes, sliced

1 sprig fresh dill, finely chopped

freshly ground black pepper, to taste

¼ cup prepared French dressing

Arrange tomato slices on serving plate. Sprinkle with dill and pepper. Serve drizzled with French dressing.

SERVES 6

GAZPACHO

2 pounds tomatoes, peeled, seeded and chopped

½ cucumber, seeded and diced

3 to 4 cloves garlic, finely chopped

4 scallions, finely sliced

½ green pepper, diced

3 tablespoons olive oil

1 to 3 tablespoons white wine vinegar

freshly ground black pepper

Tabasco sauce, to taste

4 tablespoons chopped parsley

2½ cups ice water

Dill Tomatoes

½ cucumber, seeded and diced

½ green pepper, diced

3 slices whole wheat bread, diced

1 Combine tomatoes, cucumber, garlic, scallions, green pepper, oil, vinegar, ground pepper, Tabasco sauce and parsley. Chill well. Just before serving stir through ice water.

2 Serve soup in chilled bowls. Place cucumber, diced pepper and bread in small bowls. Guests can help themselves to garnish as liked.

NOTE: 2 hard-boiled eggs can be chopped and offered as another garnish.

SERVES 10 TO 12

PATAFLA

1 baguette or other long French loaf

6 tomatoes, peeled and chopped

1 onion, thinly chopped

6 scallions, finely chopped

2 green peppers, diced

1 red pepper, diced

½ pound black olives, pitted and chopped

4 gherkins, chopped

4 tablespoons capers

4 tablespoons olive oil

freshly ground black pepper, to taste

1 Halve the loaf lengthwise. Scoop out soft interior. Crumble into a bowl with vegetables, olives, gherkins and capers. Beat mixture well. Stir in oil and pepper.

2 Divide tomato mixture between 2 bread halves. Reassemble, wrapping firmly in foil. Refrigerate overnight. Cut into thin slices to serve.

SERVES 10 TO 12

STUFFED GREEN PEPPERS

2 tablespoons butter or margarine

1 pound ground meat

1 onion, chopped

½ cup long grain rice, cooked

1 carrot, scraped and julienned

8 green peppers

4 tomatoes

3 tablespoons sour cream

1 Heat butter in a pan. Sauté ground meat, onion, rice and carrot until meat is cooked (about 20 minutes). Add a little water to mixture if necessary and simmer another 5 to 10 minutes.

2 Cut tops off peppers and carefully scoop out seeds and membranes. Spoon prepared stuffing into peppers. Place in a greased casserole dish.

3 Immerse tomatoes in hot water for about 5 minutes then hold under running cold water. Remove tomato skins. Place tomatoes in a dish.

4 Break the tomatoes with a fork and spoon pulp over the peppers. Bake, covered, in a 350°F oven for about 1 hour.

5 To serve, add sour cream to the sauce left in the pan and reheat.

SERVES 4 TO 8

 STIR-FRYING

If you are directed to stir-fry and you don't have a wok, don't worry! All you need is a deep frying pan — stir and toss over a high heat.

AVOCADO MOUSSE

3 tablespoons gelatin soaked in ⅓ cup cold water

⅓ cup boiling chicken stock

2 cups avocado purée

1 teaspoon onion juice

2 teaspoons Worcestershire sauce

½ cup mayonnaise

½ cup cream, lightly whipped

SALAD

2 small green peppers, blanched and shredded

black olives, halved and stoned

red pimiento threads

3 tablespoons prepared vinaigrette dressing

1 Oil a 6-cup ring mold.

2 Dissolve the soaked gelatin in boiling stock. Whisk into the avocado purée with onion juice and Worcestershire sauce. Set aside to cool.

3 When cold, fold in mayonnaise and lightly whipped cream. Pour into the prepared mold. Place in the refrigerator to set.

4 TO PREPARE SALAD: Lightly toss peppers, olives and pimiento threads in vinaigrette dressing.

5 To serve, unmold mousse on a platter and fill center with salad vegetables.

SERVES 4 TO 6

AVOCADO AND MANGO SHELLS

3 slices thick bacon, chopped

2 mangoes, peeled and chopped

½ cup walnut halves

½ lettuce, washed and shredded

2 avocados, seeded, halved, and flesh scooped out and diced, reserve shells

½ cup vinaigrette dressing

1 Fry bacon until crisp. Drain on absorbent paper.

2 Combine bacon, mango slices, walnuts, shredded lettuce and chunks of diced avocado. Toss gently with vinaigrette dressing.

3 Spoon salad into avocado shells and serve.

SERVES 4

PEPERONATA

⅓ cup olive oil

2 onions, sliced

2 cloves garlic, crushed

2 bay leaves, crushed

2 pounds peppers in mixed colors, thickly sliced

freshly ground black pepper

4 tomatoes, peeled, seeded and chopped

1 Heat oil in a heavy skillet. Sauté the onions and garlic with the crushed bay leaves.

2 When the onion is starting to color, add the peppers and season to taste. Continue to sauté for another 10 minutes on moderate heat.

3 Stir in the tomatoes. Cover with a lid. Continue cooking until the pepper is soft and the tomatoes have formed a thick sauce. Serve hot or cold.

SERVES 4

Avocado and Mango Shells

GROWING YOUR OWN

When it comes to vegetables, fresh is best. And the freshest come from the home garden. This chapter looks at planting a vegetable garden at the right time, in the best possible soil, with plenty of sunlight for vegetables all year round and ending up with a successful harvest.

The secret of growing home garden vegetables successfully is to understand their special requirements for cold and warm areas. Many vegetable crops fail simply because they are planted out of season.

Cool season vegetables grow best at temperatures around 50°F to 68°F or even lower and are usually resistant to frost. Plant broad beans, broccoli, Brussels sprouts, cauliflower, kohlrabi, onions, peas, spinach, turnips and rutabagas in early spring after danger of frost to the young seedlings is passed, or in late summer for fall or winter harvest. For greater accuracy, check the frost tables in your area.

Warm season vegetables like much higher temperatures (68°F to 90°F) and may tolerate even hotter weather. They will grow poorly at low temperatures and are all susceptible to frost damage. The most important warm season vegetables are beans, peppers, eggplant, okra, potato, sweet corn, sweet potato, tomato and the vine crops (chayote, cucumber, summer squash, squash, pumpkin). In mild and cold climates they are planted in spring or early summer to grow during the warmer months. In the South, many can be grown throughout the year.

Beet, cabbage, carrot, celery, endive, leek, lettuce, parsnip, radish, rhubarb, Swiss chard, scallions and Belgian endive have intermediate temperature

requirements. Some root crops may 'bolt' or run to seed if sown too late in the fall or winter or too early in the spring. Some varieties of lettuce will run to seed if sown in warm weather, so it is important to select sure-heading varieties for summer sowing.

SOIL AND WATER

It is not necessary to have different soils for different vegetables. A soil that yields choice tomatoes should also yield choice cabbages, carrots and pumpkins. The ideal soil for vegetables should have a loose crumbly texture for aeration and drainage, but should also be able to hold water and nutrients. Improve sandy soils with animal manure, vermiculite or peatmoss. Clay soils are improved by adding organic matter and coarse sand.

The quantity of water and the frequency of watering depends on the water-holding capacity of the soil. Clay soils hold water well, sandy soils poorly. Watering also depends on the depth to which the roots of different vegetables grow, the stage of growth and the weather conditions. Never wait until vegetables start wilting before watering, for they do not take kindly to 'on-off' treatment. If the soil is dry just below the surface, then it is time to water again. Early morning or evening is best for watering vegetables,

avoiding the high evaporation of the middle of the day.

Mulching is another way of conserving soil moisture. The best mulches for vegetable gardens are garden compost, leaf mold, well-rotted manure or dry grass clippings.

For most vegetables, including root crops, dig the soil to spade depth (8 to 10 inches) but do not bring subsoil to the surface. You can improve drainage of heavy soils by raising the beds 6 to 10 inches above the surrounding level and sloping the sides of the bed to about 45 degrees.

SUNLIGHT

To grow quickly, vegetables need as much sunlight as possible, especially in winter when days are short. Avoid shade from buildings, fences, shrubs or trees. On level sites run the vegetables in a north-south direction. On sloping sites run the beds across the slope.

Always plant tall vegetables such as sweet corn or tomatoes in such a way as to prevent shading low-growing crops. When growing seedlings, expose them to sunlight as soon as they emerge, otherwise they can become tall and spindly. A few vegetables and herbs such as chayote, leeks, mint, parsley and rhubarb will tolerate some shade.

WIND PROTECTION

Wind damages the leaves and stems of vegetables and weakens the root systems. Cold winds will slow growth and hot winds evaporate water from plants and the soil surface. Protect by planting trees, shrubs, hedges or timber wind breaks. Artificial wind breaks also provide support for climbing beans, cucumbers and climbing peas.

CONTAINER VEGETABLES

Growing vegetables in containers has a special appeal for people who live in apartments or townhouses, where space is limited. Tubs, pots and troughs offer a simple solution for providing every home with some fresh vegetables.

Relatively inexpensive, lightweight containers, 'easy to apply' fertilizers and the development of early maturing, compact vegetable cultivars have helped to create this interesting and rewarding hobby.

Salad vegetables — sweet pepper, carrot, cucumber, lettuce and tomato — are popular for containers because of their high quality and flavor when freshly picked. Dwarf, compact cultivars of salad vegetables and others like bush squash and zucchini are the best to choose. Small vegetables, like cress, mustard, radish, scallions and most herbs, are ideal for pot culture.

Whatever containers you choose, they must have free drainage. Container-grown vegetables cannot forage for moisture as they do in the garden. In summer, vegetables may use several times their own weight in water every day, which calls for daily watering.

Leave a space of 1–2 inches between the soil level and the rim of the container. Fill this space slowly until the water weeps from the drainage holes. This restores the soil to 'field capacity'.

INDEX

Artichokes
  and sausage fettuccine 17
  stuffed 14
Asparagus
  with herbs and parmesan 15
  and scallop bouchée 12
Avocado
  and mango shells 88
  mousse 88

Baby carrots with fresh basil 41
Baby yellow and green
    squash 63
Basil
  with baby carrots 41
  and pasta salad 52
Beans
  with almonds 22
  braised 25
  and celery salad 22
  herbed 24
  and pea soup 26
  salad 25
Beet salad, warm 37
Belgian endive with mustard
    cream 55
Belgian leek soup 75
Bread
  pan bagnia 56
  patafla 87
Broad beans, braised 25
Broccoli
  and cauliflower salad 11
  with horseradish 11
Brussels sprouts, glazed 54

Cabbage
    see also Red cabbage
  rolls 50
Cake, zucchini 68
Calamari with snow peas 26
Carrots
  baby, with fresh basil 41

and chive salad 41
  with marinated fish 36
  slice 68
Cauliflower
  and broccoli salad 11
  and macaroni soufflé 11
  pickled 12
  with tomato fettuccine
    and olives 12
Celery
  cream soup 16
  and kidney bean salad 22
  sesame braised 16
Chayote soup 61
Cheese and spinach gnocchi 52
Chicken
  cock-a-leekie 78
  and mushroom pie 43
  provençale 76
  salad, Thai 73
  soufflé roll 48
Chilled soup
  gazpacho 86
  pumpkin 63
Chinese green soup 51
Chive and carrot salad 41
Cock-a-leekie 78
Corn
  Mexican succotash 28
  on the cob, Mexican 28
  and potato puffs 29
  strudel 29
Courgette au beurre
    see Zucchini
Crab in pastry 79
Cucumber
  and mango soup 66
  stuffed 64
  and yogurt soup 66

Dhal, rosy 25
Dill
  mustard potato salad 33
  tomatoes 86
Dressing
  ginger mango 44

tahini orange 53
  tomato 24
Duck and mango combination 22

Eggplant
  moussaka 82
  with pilaf 84
  purée 82
  ratatouille 82
  ratatouille tartlets 61
Eggs with braised parsnips and
    tomatoes 38

Fennel sauté 55
Fettuccine
  artichoke and sausage 17
  with shrimp and peas 26
  tomato, with cauliflower and
    olives 12
Fish
  marinated with carrots 36
  soup, Norwegian 77

Gado-gado 41
Gazpacho 86
Ginger mango dressing 44
Glazed brussels sprouts 54
Gnocchi, cheese and spinach 52
Green beans, herbed 24
Green peppers, stuffed 87
Green salad primavera 10

Ham and split pea soup 21
Herb cream sauce 74

Kidney bean and celery
    salad 22

Lamb, rosemary, cooked on a bed
    of potatoes 39
Leeks
  cock-a-leekie soup 78
  and rice 75

roulade 79
soup, Belgian 75
vichyssoise 72
Long bean salad 25

Macaroni
  and cauliflower soufflé 11
Mango
  and avocado shells 88
  and cucumber soup 66
  and duck combination 22
  ginger dressing 44
Mexican corn on the cob 28
Mexican succotash 28
Middle Eastern Pilaf 16
Minestrone soup 21
Moussaka 82
Mushrooms
  and chicken pie 43
  caps, grilled 42
  and pork with ginger mango
    dressing 44
  soup, sherried 45
  stuffed 45
  tarragon, à la grecque 45
Mussels
  pizzaiola 83
  and snow peas 24

Norwegian fish soup 77

Okra casserole 61
Omelet, Spanish 32
Onions
  pickled 76
  ragout 73
Orange
  and spinach salad 54
  tahini dressing 53

Pan bagnia 56
Parsley and walnut soup 72
Parsnips
  braised with chopped eggs and
    tomatoes 38

with herbs 39
Pasta and basil salad 52
Pastry shells for vegetables 60
Patafla 87
Pâté, vegetable 20
Peas
    see also Split pea
  with shrimp and fettuccine 26
Peperonata 88
Peppers
  peperonata 88
  stuffed 87
Pickle
  cauliflower 12
  onions 76
  chicken and mushroom 43
  pumpkin 69
Pilaf
  with eggplant 84
  Middle Eastern 16
Piroshki 34
Pissaladiere 75
Pizzaiola mussels 83
Pork and mushrooms with ginger
    mango dressing 44
Potatoes
  and corn puffs 29
  patties 32
  piroshki 34
  with rosemary lamb 39
  salad, dill-mustard 33
  Swedish hasselback 37
  Spanish omelet 32
  sticks 37
  stuffed 38
Provençale chicken 76
Pumpkin
  chilled soup 63
  pie 69
  timbales 67
  triangles 64

Quiche, scallop and spinach 49

Radishes with sour cream 40
Ratatouille 82
  tartlets 61

Red cabbage
  nut slaw with tahini orange
    dressing 53
  with sour cream 55
Rice
    see also Pilaf
  and leeks 75
Rosemary lamb cooked on a bed of
    potatoes 39
Rosy dhal 25

Salad
  basil and pasta 52
  carrot and chive 41
  cauliflower and broccoli 11
  celery and kidney bean 22
  dill-mustard potato 33
  exotic flower 57
  gado-gado 41
  niçoise 56
  orange and spinach 54
  primavera 10
  red cabbage nut slaw with tahini
    orange dressing 53
  spirali and zucchini 61
  tartlets, whole wheat 15
  Thai chicken 73
  tuna, with garlic toast 85
  warm beet 37
Scallop
  and asparagus bouchée 12
  bundles
    with herb cream sauce 74
  and spinach quiche 49
Seafood and snow pea
    tempura 22
Sherried mushroom soup 45
Shrimp
  with peas and fettuccine 26
Slice, succulent carrot 68
Snow peas
  with calamari 26
  and mussels 24
  and seafood tempura 22
Sorrel soup 51
Soufflé
  cauliflower and macaroni 11

chicken roll 48
tofu spinach 51
Soup
  see also Chilled soup
  bean and pea 26
  Belgian leek 75
  celery cream 16
  Chinese green 51
  cock-a-leekie 78
  cream of chayote 61
  cream of spinach 48
  fresh tomato 84
  minestrone 21
  Norwegian fish 77
  parsley and walnut 72
  sherried mushroom 45
  sorrel 51
  split pea and ham 21
  tangy mango and cucumber 66
  vichyssoise 72
  yogurt and cucumber 66
Spanish omelet 32
Spinach
  and cheese gnocchi 52
  and orange salad 54
  and scallop quiche 49
  soup 48
  tofu soufflé 51
Spirali
  and zucchini salad 62

Split pea
  and bean soup 26
  and ham soup 21
Squash
  baby yellow and green 63
  stuffed 65
String beans with almonds 22
Strudel
  sweet corn 29
  vegetable 27
Succotash, Mexican 28
Swedish hasselback potatoes 37
Sweet corn *see* Corn
Sweet potatoes, scalloped 32

Tahini orange dressing 53
Tarragon mushrooms
  à la grecque 45
Tarts
  ratatouille 61
  scallop and spinach
    quiche 49
  shells for vegetables 60
  whole wheat salad 15
Tempura
  snow pea and seafood 22
Thai chicken salad 73
Timbales, pumpkin 67
Tofu spinach soufflé 51

Tomato fettuccine with cauliflower
    and olives 12
Tomatoes
  with braised parsnips and
    chopped eggs 38
  dill 86
  dressing 24
  gazpacho 86
  persilles 84
  soup 84
Tuna salad with garlic toast 85
Turnips, baked 41

Vichyssoise 72

Warm salad, beet 37
Whole wheat salad tartlets 15

Yogurt and cucumber soup 66

Zucchini
  au beurre 63
  baked, in sour cream 63
  cake 68
  and spirali salad 62
  ratatouille tartlets 61